GROW!

ALSO BY TREVOR SILVESTER:

Lovebirds
How to Click

TREVOR SILVESTER

GROW!

Personal Development
for Parents

CORONET

First published in Great Britain in 2017 by Coronet
An imprint of Hodder & Stoughton
An Hachette UK company

1

Copyright © Trevor Silvester 2017

The right of Trevor Silvester to be identified as
the Author of the Work has been asserted by him in accordance
with the Copyright, Designs and Patents Act 1988.

A CIP catalogue record for this title
is available from the British Library

Paperback ISBN: 978 1 444 74090 5
Ebook ISBN: 978 1 444 74091 2

Typeset in Sabon MT by Palimpsest Book Production Ltd,
Falkirk, Stirlingshire

Printed and bound by Clays Ltd, St Ives plc

Hodder & Stoughton policy is to use papers that are natural,
renewable and recyclable products and made from wood grown in
sustainable forests. The logging and manufacturing processes are
expected to conform to the environmental regulations
of the country of origin.

Hodder & Stoughton Ltd
Carmelite House
50 Victoria Embankment
London EC4Y 0DZ

www.hodder.co.uk

To my family. Past, present and future

Contents

Introduction   1

PART I: THIS IS ALL ABOUT YOU

CHAPTER 1: It's not what happens to you   13
CHAPTER 2: Our culture's toxins   37

PART II: GROWING A BETTER 'YOU'

LESSON 1: Be ILOC   51
LESSON 2: You can believe what suits you best   77
LESSON 3: You can choose who you want to be   84

PART III: GROWING YOUR CHILD

8 Mantras for parents

MANTRA 1: You're training them or they're training you   101
MANTRA 2: They're not who they're going to be yet   107
MANTRA 3: Rewards don't always reward them   112
MANTRA 4: It's good to give them less   121
MANTRA 5: Life is what you make it mean   126

MANTRA 6: They're not difficult, they're just not you   138
MANTRA 7: Growing ILOC children takes bravery   170
MANTRA 8: Don't expect   180

PART IV: GROWING THROUGH THE AGES

Growing through the ages   193
Pregnancy   193
0–7 years   197
7–12 years   205
12 to adult   213

A letter to young people: 220
Seven things I want you to know
- Bad things are going to happen to you
- You feed what you focus on
- Sometimes your fears don't matter, or aren't even yours
- You get the future you expect
- Nobody is worth knowing who thinks what you wear matters
- Sometimes what others try to teach you is because of their own stuff
- You're writing your life story. Be the character in it you want to be.

Conclusion   241
Bibliography   243
Acknowledgements   245

Introduction

If parenthood doesn't scare you, you probably aren't one. To bring into the world a little person who is utterly reliant on you, but who, with every passing day, seems to deviate more and more from your ideas about what's best for them, is a challenge that evolves as the years go by yet somehow never diminishes. It's also an unequalled opportunity to do good for the child and for the parents to do some good for themselves.

I'm going to teach you how to raise your child so they have the kind of attitude towards life that will make them resilient in the face of its many challenges and free of the limitations that hold so many people back. But I'm also going to teach you a bit about you – because how can you expect to raise a child a certain way without becoming more that way yourself? Gandhi once said, 'Be the change you want to see in the world.' I'm going to paraphrase the great man and say, 'Be the change you want to see in your children.'

This is a book of four parts. In the first part I'm going to explain what your brain is doing to create the version of the world you live in and the kind of person you believe yourself to be. I'm going to describe how a glitch in the survival software that's protected us for millions of years can lead to beliefs about our self, and the world, that limit us and make ourselves our own worst enemy.

In the second part I teach you three lessons about how to take back control of your life, and your feelings about yourself, by developing a new mindset that inoculates you from the pressures of pleasing society and gives you back the power to choose the life you want to live.

These first two parts are about you, the adult, but you'll see that what you learn about yourself will be applicable to how you parent your children. In Part III we focus on that specifically. I give you eight parenting mantras and explain why integrating them into your everyday connection to your children will help them grow into strong, happy adults.

Part IV begins with looking at developmental stages in children, and tailors advice to what might aid you at particular moments in your children's life. I then go on to talk to the children themselves. It's ideas and thoughts that I've gathered from twenty years of listening to people's problems and thirty years of being a parent. While it's written to the children, I think you'll find I'm speaking to you at the same time, so don't feel that you're eavesdropping.

I've written this book for parents without presenting myself as any kind of expert on children. What I am is a therapist with a perspective that I hope you'll find useful.

The scary news is that, while I've listened to many harrowing tales of abuse, neglect and harm, much more often the source of a client's misery has arisen from a misinterpretation of more everyday contacts with their parents, siblings, friends, or other significant figures. So many times I've found myself recognising similar interactions from my own youth, or – more uncomfortably – those between me and my own children. I'm including scientific findings that support my opinions whenever I have them, but I haven't limited what I say to what I can prove. Like every other bit of advice you'll get about being a parent I trust you'll absorb what you find useful and rightfully discard what you don't.

The central theme of the book is that living things are in one of two biological states: *growth* or *protection*. I'm going to suggest that a lot of what your brain spends its day doing is working out, moment to moment, which state you should be in, and that it uses our memories to guide its decisions. Cumulatively, such decisions guide each of us towards a tendency to interpret the world, and what happens to us, in one or other of those two ways most of the time – *we see the world as a place we need to protect ourselves from or we see it as a place where we can thrive.* What this means is that decisions we make as children about the meanings of our parents shouting at us; or splitting up; or seeming to favour a sibling; or our feeling stupid in front of our friends or rejected by them; or humiliated by a teacher, can be the beginning of a chain of interpretations or misinterpretations that lead us into being in a state of protection unnecessarily. Does this matter? Hell yes. Not only can the physical state of protection lead to major health problems, it colours every relationship you have, every goal you pursue, and every interaction you share.

In a world where you're primed for attack, everyone is a possible attacker and threat is contained in every opportunity. I'm going to argue that a life lived in protection as a default state is the result of not liking who you are and that living in growth arises from a strong sense of having fun just being you.

My purpose in writing this book is to establish these two positions of growth and protection as a principle in parenting and to help answer questions about *what will help your children grow and what will prevent them from getting triggered into a state of unnecessary protection.*

How can you ensure your child grows up liking him- or herself and doesn't become someone who fears rejection, or failure, or never feels good enough? My answers are here. They apply to you as well, because it's hard to raise a child in growth if you're in protection. Sometimes I'll be talking about how you relate to your children and sometimes how you relate to yourself. As part of that I have to wonder who you, the parents, are? I mean, I'm sitting in front of my computer and I've put a pile of blank paper beside me. That's the book we're both just beginning. I want to write something that helps you to guide your children towards a happy life but also helps you along the way to do the same; so I need to know who you are, don't I? That's not easy when there could be a million of you – at least if the publisher's dreams come true. So let me take a stab at describing you. You're probably between 15 and 115, male or female, gay, straight, or somewhere in-between. You're in a relationship, were in one, want to be in one, or you've vowed to be on your own for ever. How am I doing? I know, it's years of experience.

Let me drill a bit deeper: you sometimes have a feeling that you are capable of more than you're achieving, that something in you is waiting to be revealed to the world. You're not always sure that people like you, and you're not always secure in the love of those who should. There are times when you worry about being good enough. Sometimes you even wonder if you deserve success or happiness as much as other people. Probably not all of these apply to you, but a couple will have made you nod, however slowly or grudgingly. I'll keep going. You had a childhood that contained some events that left a mark and which sometimes still hold you back. You've been hurt in love and maybe still hope for a relationship that makes you whole. Maybe you're even increasingly feeling that you don't quite belong in the culture that surrounds you. You're looking to fill something of a void in your life in a better way than you've managed to date. To be honest, life is sometimes a bit of a struggle for you.

How do I know? Because the feelings I've described seem almost universal. I've heard combinations of these feelings coming from everybody sitting opposite me in my clinic, or at dinner parties, or in conversations overheard on the train. I cannot tell you how liberating it was for me to hear these things coming from the mouths of others. They were an echo of the thoughts I held in my own secret places. What was liberating was the knowledge that I wasn't alone.

These thoughts connect the poor to the rich, the young to the old, the genders, sexual orientations, and races. **We're all fellow strugglers.**

It's what we do within our heads that causes the struggle. Our thoughts, beliefs, feelings and values create a world around us that enables us to thrive or to wilt. Often we feel a victim of them. I want to talk to you, to let you know what I know, to let you know what I want my kids and your kids to know: that you can make yourself into the person you set your mind to becoming and you can help your children do that too. While the focus of this book is on parenting it also applies to your life – **none of us are who we're going to be yet;** it's just that, **left to itself, our brain tends to keep making us more of what we've always been.** And while that's change of a kind, it may not serve you. There are things you can think, and things you can do, that can turn you into the creator of your life and not just the helpless created. If you're not having fun just being you, this book can help to change that. And a parent having fun being themselves is a parent who will raise their child in growth. There are things to do, and things to avoid, that will encourage your children to grow productively. Through sharing the most valuable things I've learnt from my years of being a therapist, I hope to avoid your children ever needing one. I'm going to take you on a journey through a series of life lessons. I'm going to give you the chance to try them out in your own life and see the difference they make to you and yours. But they come with a warning. If you truly live what this book teaches you, things will change. You will lose things from your life – your excuses most of all – and you will gain things, few of them actually material. Like Neo in the film *The Matrix*, this book acts as a red pill. If you take it, you wake up in a different world – and there'll be no going back.

I should also make it clear from the beginning that a lot of what I'm saying is from my experiences of regressing clients back to childhood events. I know some people think of regression as weird or problematic. I don't. What did you have for dinner last night? You see, I just did it. Regression is the act of causing someone to bring their past to mind. We all do it every day. Regression in my therapy is simply asking the client (in a particular way) to notice what memories come to mind when their attention is on their problem. In the next chapter I'm going to explain a theory of mind and memory that suggests that how we interpret the present is a result of connections our brains find between now and events in our past. Like a string of beads, our memories connect together through the years according to the meanings our brains give them. The good news is that our memories are plastic, so old memories that cause unhappy responses in our present can be changed. We do not have to be the victims of our past. In fact, to live in a state of growth, we need to free ourselves from it. This book will give you an insight into how that is possible. The more you're free of the negative effects of your childhood the less likely you are to infect your children with them.

Let me give an example from my own childhood of a small event that had a large effect later.

When I was about eight my family wanted to get a dog. My family, that is, apart from my mum. We undertook a campaign to wear her down, but with no success – she was pretty sure who would end up doing most of the work. One day, on a journey to school with my dad, I decided to give him the benefit of my extensive experience with women, and said, 'Dad, you're the man of the house. If you want a dog you should put your foot down and say we're getting a dog.' That evening my dad took my advice. Numpty.

We lived in a council flat, so I could hear what went on in the living room from my bed. Sure enough, I heard them having another talk about getting a dog. All good so far. It became more heated. That was unusual, my parents didn't used to row much. Finally, with Dad's foot firmly down I heard my mum shout, 'Well you can have a divorce, but I'm keeping the kids!'

I remember to this day my heart freezing with the thought that I'd split the family up. I don't think I'd ever known such fear. I'm sure I had a disturbed night. Yet, when I went to breakfast the next morning, not only had they made up – but I was greeted by the news that we were getting a dog! What I discovered, through my own therapy, was that the relief of hearing this news didn't undo the moment of deep fear from the night before. My brain had stored it to keep me safe from anything that scary ever happening again. And what effect did it have?

I never felt free to say what I felt in relationships or to allow any anger to be expressed towards a partner. The techniques of Cognitive Hypnotherapy helped me to re-write that narrative – to apply to the memory of the night of the 'dog talk' my adult understanding that my mum, like many, sometimes had a tactic of pushing her point of view to an extreme to make people back away from theirs. The result has been that now it's no longer an issue for me – and if I want a dog I'll put my foot down and ask my wife really nicely.

A key thing I want to be clear about from the beginning is that I'm not saying that my report of this event is 'The Truth' about what happened, any more than my new understanding of it is. They're both just interpretations. I'm going to explain how we create a story about ourselves that builds our character and our responses to the world as a result of such interpretations. Our brain takes this story very seriously, treating it as true. It isn't. I'm going to teach you how to create a narrative for your children that leads to a happy life and, along the way, show you how to treat yourself as the author of your own story, not just a character in it. So if you want to change it – you can.

This is a very personal book that is in no way intended as a gospel, more as a tool to make you think. One of the things that makes it so personal was the news I received, shortly before I started writing, that I was to become a grandfather. While the book has grown I've watched my grandson Heath begin his life, and, as the book progressed, he has been joined by two cousins, Sasha and Seth. I'm blessed. They've been much in my mind as I've written, becoming a natural focus for what I hope this book will achieve. Maybe the ideas contained here will help to shape their journey. That's not my decision, but I do hope so.

PART I:

THIS IS ALL ABOUT YOU

The story begins: How you become who you are...

CHAPTER 1:

It's not what happens to you...

Two brothers were raised by an abusive alcoholic father who beat them regularly and took pleasure in humiliating and belittling them. When they grew to manhood one brother became the image of his father and treated his children every bit as badly. The other brother grew into a successful businessman and loving father. Someone asked each in turn, 'How did you manage to turn out this way?' Both gave the same answer, 'How could I have turned out any differently given my childhood?'

For twenty years I've sat in my therapy room and listened to people. I've heard hundreds of stories from childhood that had led to lives of pain and limitation. Some are what you'd expect – abuse, trauma and deprivation – but many are much more mundane. Can a bad first day at school really lead to a fear of failure? Can a single moment of rejection lead to serial relationship disasters? It certainly seems so. Yet for every childhood sufferer of trauma whose adult life still bears the scars, there is an adult for whom that experience has been a catalyst for creating a life of meaning and achievement.

Until its sad demise I worked as a therapist with Kids

Company, a charity that helped vulnerable young people. As a consequence, I've been a regular witness to young people dragging themselves out of a routine of deprivation to pursue a better life with a resilience that left me breathless. While in my Harley Street practice, I sometimes see clients who've lived a life of privilege who remain stuck in a gilded prison that only their thoughts have created. As with the two brothers in the story, it doesn't seem to be what happens to us that defines us anywhere near as much, or as often, as the meaning we give it. If that's true, if life is what we make it, why not make it great? If what we make of life is the result of our interpretations, how can we guide ourselves and our children towards a positive interpretation of an event rather than a negative one? How can we choose an interpretation that causes us to open up to the world and its possibilities rather than shut ourselves off, an interpretation that leads us to lead a life of growth rather than one of protection? Which brings me back to the central theme of the book.

Growth and protection

If we take one of your cells and put it in a petri dish with a source of nutrient, it will move towards the nutrient. If you replace the nutrient with a toxin, the cell will move away. In other words, the cell moves towards an opportunity for growth, or it recognises and responds to a need for protection.

As a collection of a trillion cells, I suggest we do the same thing. Freud described this as the *pleasure principle* – that we all move towards pleasure and away from pain. From day one on this planet your brain has been interpreting your experiences, using them to predict the way the world works and what is going to happen to you moment to moment. The purpose of that interpretation is to identify correctly, within any situation you face, whether protection is necessary or whether growth is possible. The more you are able to be in growth the more opportunities you're likely to have to thrive. **The key message of this book is that it can be overwhelmingly a matter of choice as to whether you spend your time in growth or protection.**

One thing I want to be clear about is this: I'm not suggesting that our protection response is the bad guy. It's played a key role in our survival as a species. Wanting to protect our children is one of the most powerful instincts we have. However, that very strength can cause us to teach our children to fear unnecessarily and even guide them into limiting beliefs about themselves that hold them back their whole life. Through reading this book you may come to realise that the same has happened to you. This book is about learning to distinguish unnecessary protection from actual threats. It's about how to let go of the limitations you experience and foster a mindset that seeks growth and a life of happiness, fulfilment and achievement.

Learning begins sooner than you think

From the moment a baby is born, its brain gets busy trying to figure out where it's landed. Like a paratrooper dropped into enemy territory it comes equipped with everything that previous paratroopers have found useful to help them survive. It then keeps what it finds useful and discards what it doesn't. For example, all babies smile but if they get no response from it they stop doing it. For ever. It just disappears. Interestingly, anything that counts as a good response – what in psychology they call a positive stroke – like cooing, hugging or tickling maintains baby's ability to smile.

A baby's responses to the world around her – what she does more or less of – are guided by software that organises and interprets the information flowing through her senses. It's kept busy. I've read estimates that suggest that between seven and eleven million bits of information move through our sense organs every second – simply too much for any brain to process. A famous piece of research concluded that we can only attend consciously to roughly seven bits of information at a time. You read that right, seven bits out of eleven million. You're probably wondering how on earth the brain decides which seven bits they should be. What is the software looking for? It's looking for whether a protection response is required, or what actions will best lead to growth. That's what our software is doing when it sorts through the eleven million bits of information every second and leaves us with just seven to pay attention to: figuring out what is relevant to our growth or protection and what isn't. But how can it possibly know?

The short answer to that question is memory.

Memory – the remembered present

The fact that we have a memory raises an interesting question. Do you remember your wedding day? Or the worst day of your life (I'm hoping they were different days)? When you think about it, *what's the point of being able to recall them?*

There is growing evidence to suggest that our memory exists to make sense of the present. Some 80% of what we see around us is actually information that we are projecting. When we look at something we are not seeing it just as it is but with layers of personal interpretation added. If you look at an apple it's easy to miss the fact that it comes with an attitude towards it – do you like them or hate them? Prefer red to green? Sliced and peeled or straight off the tree? Does it remind you of Snow White or William Tell? That day you choked on a bite or hit a friend on the back of the head with a core? An apple is an apple until we look at it, then it becomes *our* version of an apple.

This is why we have different tastes, styles, preferences. It's why you can't see what your friend finds attractive in their partner. These layers are provided by our memory.

We've learned what we like and don't like. We evolve an attitude to things over a lifetime.

Your brain is constantly shuttling backwards into the past to look for relationships between what's happening to you now and what happened before. It then uses the connections it finds to predict what is likely to happen to you next. If your brain finds a connection between a current event and an event in the past that was interpreted by your brain as a negative, it will imagine a negative consequence coming your way. To defend you from that it triggers a protection response, which takes control of your actions away from you and goes through a predictable series of behaviours designed to help (basically, variations on a theme of aggression, avoidance or freezing), even if they actually don't.

In the event of a threat, the brain has at its disposal what I'll be referring to as the *protection system*. It kicks in with one of three responses whenever the brain perceives an imminent danger. You get ready to fight, to run away, or to freeze. To get us to do those things hormones are released to raise our blood pressure so you tend to shake; your respiration increases to feed more oxygen into your muscles so you breathe more quickly; your body temperature increases because your muscles are more efficient if they're warm (so you sweat); and blood is diverted from the stomach to get the oxygen to the muscles you fight or run away with – hence that feeling you get in your stomach, referred to in my family as the collywobbles. Finally, if the threat is strong enough, blood flow is reduced to the part of the brain that deals with our higher level thinking and planning. This is because our protection system evolved mainly to deal with things trying to eat us, and thinking can slow down our responses. As a result, there is a maxim that tends to hold true: **strong emotions make us stupid.**

If, on the other hand, your brain connects your present situation to a positive past event, it predicts a pleasant impending future and switches to another system – *the reward system.* This releases dopamine into your brain which yields a nice feeling that motivates you to seek more of it.

In very simple terms, these are the two chemical systems that power the direction our life takes from moment to moment. Under ideal circumstances we'd live a life of pure growth, where we're nourished, encouraged, loved, and supported by everybody we meet. Our young brain would interpret everything that happens to us in a way that predicts more good things to come. Nothing would ever threaten us or make us feel insecure. It's dopamine heaven. Hands up whose life I've just described? That's right, nobody's.

If we're lucky we get a mixture. Good things happen to us, bad things happen to us, and lots of stuff in-between. In the main, the good things get reinforced so we grow up motivated to do things we've learned we're good at and the bad things that happen to us give us some healthy protection responses that keep us away from genuinely bad stuff. But, even if you're this lucky, your brain will still have made some errors of understanding or come to wrong conclusions along the way.

Whatever their source, all of us have got some software errors in our programming. Some will be because we were fed rubbish peddled as truth by people older than us, like my mother telling me when I was growing up that any behaviour of mine she didn't like was against the law. Some errors will come from our own mistakes in interpreting what's happening to us or around us. Bear in mind, if you're a parent, that you're sometimes going to be the deliverer of the things that lead to your children's miscalculations. Sometimes this is because they misunderstand what you say or do, sometimes because you spoke out of anger, fear or frustration, and sometimes because you're passing on the rubbish you haven't sorted yourself. Some of these miscalculations will be inconsequential and others will shape your children and their lives. The difficult thing is, you're not going to know which is which. Things you thought were big deals will be forgotten by your kids. Things you thought were trivial will stick in their heads. It's why no kid gets out of childhood without issues, and why we, as parents, need to forget about trying to raise our children perfectly and stop beating ourselves up when we don't.

What we do vs. who we are

I once had a client called Lisa who came to see me complaining of low self-esteem. When clients first start describing their problems of low confidence they usually generalise by saying, 'I have no confidence'. This is very rarely entirely true. When I probe it becomes more defined, more contextual. 'There are times when I lack confidence' is a very different proposition to 'I have no confidence'. The brain has this trick of taking the things we don't do well and applying them to who we feel ourselves to be. What should be, 'Sometimes I act stupidly' comes out as 'I'm stupid'. 'I get tongue-tied in company' is expressed as 'I'm boring'. **We confuse what we do with who we are.** What I've found is that it's much easier to help people change what they consider to be something they *do*, compared to something they consider they *are*. We all tend to hold on to beliefs about our identity quite fiercely, even if they make us unhappy.

In this case, Lisa's issue began with 'I'm not good enough', and was causing anxiety about being able to keep her job. With some questioning, the context was narrowed to certain times at work: 'I often feel inferior to the people around me at work. I know I know as much as them, but something stops me from contributing in meetings or putting myself forward for promotion.' In therapy I use a technique to help people follow their story backwards to find the root of their issue. Lisa identified that the problem began at about eight years old when she was at school. A teacher asked her to stand up and answer a question. Because she was an introvert (who tend to hate performing in front of others) this was a bit of a challenge. She got flustered, turned red, and started stuttering. Her classmates began to titter. Unfortunately, her teacher was one of those who shouldn't be. He harangued her for being stupid. Not surprisingly, the answer she finally managed to dredge up was completely wrong, which led to even more amusement from her 'friends' and more contempt from the teacher. Lisa ran out crying. In my line of work, we call this a Significant Emotional Event (SEE). In a negative context, it's a moment when our brains strongly identify a threat to us, physically or socially – fear of rejection being a big example of the latter. In a positive context, our brain recognises a growth opportunity and motivates us to seek more of the same experiences. Growing confidence and self-regard are usual consequences of these.

When an SEE occurs, the brain takes a low resolution 'photograph' that traps information from all five senses. This is used by our memory as a source of comparison between it and experiences we have later. So, with Lisa, anything that was present in the moment of this first SEE, the incident at school, could cause a later event to be connected to it – e.g. people looking at her; an authority figure asking her a question; potentially, even the colour of the walls. It's a bit like a game of snap. Each moment of your life is a card the brain compares to the set of SEE cards it holds. If it decides there's a match, it shouts 'Snap!' If it's a protection card it prompts you into a protection response. If it's a growth card (a positive SEE) it will prompt you into a growth response. In Lisa's case, all of the situations suggested as matches to the initial event would be perceived as threatening. The brain's response to a threat is to swing in with the protection response, to get us to fight, run, as in Lisa's case, or to freeze. The problem is that **when a negative emotion, like a fear of looking stupid, is driving our actions, it tends to lead to the very thing we're trying to avoid.**

An example is a woman who came to see me with a history of broken relationships. We identified that she had a belief that she's unlovable. Any time she got into a relationship she expected to be rejected. Her response to this fear was to be over-affectionate, clingy and jealous. Every time she drove her man away through her attempts to keep him. Another example is a man who believes that he's not good enough. To compensate he works incredibly hard at his job but, because of his self-doubt, he checks and double-checks everything. He falls behind with his deadlines, is indecisive, and micro manages his staff. The productivity of his department falls and he loses his job, which reinforces his original belief that he wasn't good enough.

I sometimes call SEEs 'butterfly' events after the 'butterfly effect' – the idea that a butterfly flapping its wings in the Amazon can cause a storm in Australia a month later. In something as complex as the weather, or the brain, something small can have an amplifying effect as time goes by. What can begin as a relatively minor event in childhood can grow into something really significant by adulthood. The more something happens the more our brain believes it will happen again.

In non-SEE situations, the brain will update early decisions based on what it learns further down the line. For example, I regularly walk into a room full of people waiting for me to teach them. As I walk in I experience a feeling of excitement and, well, happiness. That wasn't always true. When I first started teaching, my legs used to literally shake on the way to the classroom. I loved teaching from the beginning, but walking into a room of people and being the focus of attention was a challenge. I won't have been alone in that. A survey showed that the greatest fear Americans suffered from was a fear of public speaking, followed by a fear of death. As Seinfeld remarked, it suggested that the person giving the eulogy at a funeral would rather be the one in the box. My brain was clearly making something threatening out of the contents of a classroom. Later, as I got used to teaching, my brain didn't create the same response. Why did my brain update my experience when Lisa's didn't? It seems that when an experience is registered as a butterfly event, its purpose is to 'fix' your response. Your brain would rather you take the same mistaken action a hundred times, than fail to respond once to the danger the SEE represents. My initial fear in front of a group is likely to have been solely a natural consequence of being an introvert. It wasn't compounded by an SEE as in Lisa's situation, so my brain was able to update the meaning of the experience positively as I relaxed and gained confidence. **Sometimes, as in Lisa's case, our past keeps happening to us. That doesn't have to be the case. We have ways of undoing past learning.**

The Christian idea that man is born sinful has influenced our culture for rather a long time. We easily absorb the idea that there is something inherently wrong with us. Freud's spin on things didn't help. The idea that we have this nasty, unconscious Id fighting for expression, waiting to leap out and do ghastly things when the Ego's back is turned, turns life into an ongoing battle within ourselves. I'm suggesting something fundamentally very different. I am suggesting **we are born to grow.**

All you need is love

Gil Boyne, with over fifty years of clinical experience, was one of the most famous hypnotherapists of the twentieth century. Back in the mid-1970s, he helped a struggling young actor called Sylvester Stallone with writer's block. He went on to write *Rocky* a few months later. I was lucky enough to have Gil as a mentor and friend. Over the course of his clinical career he came to the conclusion that the human race suffers from a universal limiting belief that we all seem to pick up in childhood to some degree or other: that *we are unloved or unlovable.*

I resisted his conclusion for many years. Nowadays, I find it hard to argue with because I see it so often, not just in my clients, but in the people I come across in everyday life.

Our protection response has evolved to deal with the threats our ancestors faced for millions of years. These threats come in two main flavours. The first is the obvious, *physical threats to our life*. The second is threats to our *social wellbeing*. When you look at us, we're actually quite puny in relation to the things that were hunting us, or even that we were hunting. Really, we should have been easy meat. What saved us was our big brain. It allowed us the scope to cooperate and collaborate with others, which levelled the killing field. As roaming bands of hunter-gatherers, we learned to get along and thrived as a consequence. We also learned that not getting along, not bonding with your tribe, not having people care about you, led to exclusion and inevitable death. The more highly valued you were or the more loved by others you were, the closer to the warmth of the fire you sat, the bigger slice of the carcass you dined on and the greater selection of mates you had. Our social standing was a big deal. It still is.

How we scale the slippery slope of social approval and collect love from others begins within hours of birth. One of the first things your child learns to do is to recognise faces. In particular, the faces of those around them who are most likely to nourish and protect them. They learn what entertains the nurturers and keeps the nurture coming. Babies learned early there were no social services in the Neolithic age, so they became geniuses at being cute and endearing. They're basically trying to be love magnets.

Children quickly gain a sensitivity to their place in their social world. They learn which behaviours gain approval (more love) from their parents, and which cause approval to be withdrawn or punishment to be administered (not loved, in a child's simple way of figuring things). Children can be taught that *any* behaviour is good or bad depending on how it is rewarded or punished. We all know that children can be led into doing horrible things in order to feel loved or accepted.

Later, this search for acceptance and love continues with our peers. Watch children play. Child's play is the last thing it is; it's a complex and subtle exchange of cues that establishes roles and pecking order. Above all else, the thing children want to avoid is rejection from their group, which is one reason why it's been so easy for manufacturers to link a child's self-esteem to the labels they wear. The one thing they mustn't be is different to their group, because, as we've seen, at a primeval level, difference is dangerous. Back in the day, other clans and tribes represented a potential danger and competition for our resources. All primitive tribes, from the Toulambi in New Guinea to Arsenal football supporters, dress to distinguish themselves from others. They develop their own songs and chants; their own traditions. It's not so different with our children and it's for the same reason: to create a sense of belonging and cohesion within the group. Within that group emerges a hierarchy based around whatever each group learns to value. Once it might have been hunting or cooking prowess. Now, among teens . . . I don't know . . . texting speed, the number of Bieber posters on their wall? And it's the same for us adults. From babyhood onwards, we pursue actions that we've learned bring us social reward (love, in Gil's terms) and avoid things that cause us to be rejected – first from our parents and then, later, our friends, peers and colleagues.

We tend to get the future we expect

Suppose, when you're five years old, you're picked to be the Christmas fairy in the school nativity play. It's your big moment and, at the urging of your teacher, you scamper up the steps to the stage in your tutu. Unfortunately, you catch your foot on the top step and enter stage left sliding on your belly with your wand flying into the audience – who duly laugh. A lot. Now, this is one of those 'two brothers' moments. One child might see the mortified look of her mother and interpret it as disapproval of her clumsiness. She feels embarrassed at the laughter. Her brain stores the event as something to be avoided in the future. Subsequently, any situation involving her being observed by other people is matched to this butterfly event (or SEE) and a similar disaster is predicted. The protection response is fired. Her life grows into one where performing or speaking up in front of others is avoided at all costs. Each similar event gets connected to the events before. The negative anticipation is amplified from each reinforcement. That, unfortunately, was my client's interpretation. But it wasn't the only one available to her.

An alternative could have been: she finished sliding, saw people laughing and interpreted that as approval. The memory was stored as a positive butterfly event. From then on, in anticipation of a speaking opportunity, when her brain asked 'What's that going to be like?', it connected to that first positive butterfly event – it connected to that feeling of approval. Each subsequent positive experience built on the last. This growing chain of connections led to a growing confidence about such occasions. She grew into someone who loved speaking to an audience. **Success breeds the expectation of success, just as failure breeds more of its own kind.**

Our overall level of self-confidence tends to be a balance between how many situations we have in life in which we feel positive about our competency (and the approval of others) versus how many in which we feel negative about it. Most of us will have a few situations where our confidence deserts us, some of us will have many. Some of us will judge ourselves harshly in those moments of desertion, others will be more forgiving.

For each singular episode like the one described above, there will be a million smaller versions in-between. Each subsequent event, matched to the original, has the potential to enhance the response in a lesser or greater way, to add a variation to the context or to dampen it. I've listened to clients' life stories where a similar incident has led to a fear of exams, of public speaking, of meeting people, of being wrong – the list is extensive, but connected by a single organising drive – a fear of the disapproval of others

29

or, in Gil Boyne's terms, a fear of the withdrawal of love. Ultimately, a single occasion can lie at the heart of someone's low self-esteem.

It won't always be a single event. Just as common is the consistent drip feeding of messages we sometimes get from our parents: that somehow we're not good enough, that we never quite reach the standard they'd be happy with, that we're not what they ordered from the stork, that we're a disappointment. Sometimes, it's our misinterpretation. Sometimes, it's the result of their own personal unhappiness. They just can't keep it to themselves so it spills over onto their children, who, sadly, sometimes pass it on to theirs.

Research has shown that if a new mother had a childhood where her mother didn't create a secure attachment through the stroking and attention I spoke of earlier, it becomes much more difficult for her to provide a secure, nurturing environment for her own offspring. With clients, I often get this sense of an unhappy ancestor whose dislike of themselves has been passed down from generation to generation like an unwelcome heirloom. The source is long since lost, all that's left is the kind of family who seem to be genetically unhappy. I don't think they are, they're just being true to the introjected teaching of their parents and the parents before them. It doesn't have to be this way. If this sounds like your family, you could be the generation of parents who end that.

The course of our lives is influenced by our interpretation of what happens to us as we meander through the world –

and that interpretation is overwhelmingly unconscious. The good news is this means that the world we meander through isn't the world as it is, but the world as you make it, which means **you have the power to change it.**

Because, because, because...

Children often make mistakes as a result of miscalculations about why things happen because their brains are constantly seeking reasons:

- Because Dad snaps at them for getting their sums wrong when he comes home tired at the end of the day they conclude that they're stupid. Even worse, they conclude he doesn't love them.
- Because Mum is busy with their new baby sister she doesn't seem to spend as much time with them, unless they're ill. Having something wrong with them becomes a way of gaining attention.
- Because their parents are going through a bad patch they're short tempered and snap at them more. The child does her best to please them. When they split up the child blames herself. As she grows up, she continues to people-please in the hope of nothing else bad happening. She takes responsibility for everyone else's wellbeing.

With none of these examples am I suggesting that the conclusion the child draws is inevitable. Other children might give entirely different meanings to the situations. The thing is, you never quite know which child is coming to what conclusion. And you can't be omnipresent to guide them to the right one. It's why I say again that, as a parent, it will help if you discard the idea of raising your child without issues. Chill a little. You just never know, and can't control, what sense they're making of all the things that are going to happen to them. You just can't be perfect.

A young brain, seeking causes as it's programmed to do, still believing that everything is about them, is capable of coming to amazingly wrong conclusions.

Parenting Tip: Identify causative errors

If your child says something that indicates they're thinking or feeling for reasons of protecting themselves, like 'I'm stupid', 'I'll never be able to...', 'Nobody likes me' or 'I can't X...' gently enquire 'Because?' This will often reveal the under-lying belief that creates the effect present in their statement. Once you're aware of it, you'll find things throughout this book you can do to help 'unpick' this error.

The different ways we have of knowing we are loved

How often I've heard couples complain of each other, 'You not doing x means you don't love me', or 'I can tell she's going off me because she doesn't hug me/tell me/look at me like she used to'. In my book *Lovebirds*, I write at length about how each of us has ways of knowing we're loved. I'm mainly talking about *equivalences*, where A (a certain behaviour) = B (love).The key point here is the equivalences *you* have for love may not be the same as your partner's or your children's. You could be doing towards them everything you'd recognise as loving behaviour but still leave them feeling unloved. Meanwhile, your children are doing everything they can through their actions to elicit the missing (to them) evidence from you that you care – including behaving badly – and you might miss or misinterpret these signs completely. When I work with clients who smoke or who want to lose weight, I often notice an interesting thing: that the cigarette, or a particular food type, has an emotional equivalence, such as chocolate = love, company, comfort or rebellion. For example, how many parents reward children for good behaviour by giving them sweets? After a while the sweets can become an expression of love or approval from the parent. Fast forward twenty years to a bad day at the office where you've been shouted at. Is it any wonder that your unconscious reaches for the chocolate bar in an attempt to help you feel better about yourself?

Parenting Tip: Think about what you reward your children with

Reward a child with experiences or your time and attention, not with things like sweets or toys.

It's the same, but different

Your child is going to meet a lot of situations for which their life has no matches and their brain interprets the event incorrectly. First experiences of any kind can qualify. If you're aware that each one presents a potential moment where their young brains could default to protection simply due to being overwhelmed by the absence of recognition, then you can be ready to provide them with guidance about what the best 'grow' conclusion can be made from it. The first day at school can, out of fear, be made into loss of their mother or even rejection by her. Alternatively, it could be about the chance to make new friends and have fun. I see this very clearly with new parents and their response to the child falling over. Often the child is shocked by the suddenness of a fall and looks towards the parent. If they see the parent fearful, or panicked, or if the parent exclaims in alarm, then it's often that which will trigger a tearful response in the child. After a few experiences this is no longer a 'different' experience. It is now one for which an equivalence has been made – the feelings that come from falling are to be avoided, or are painful, or cause alarm in the parent. The child learns to either become scared of 'pain' or scared of events that might lead to it. The butterfly journey towards risk aversion and over-sensitisation to unpleasant feelings begins.

Parenting Tip: Create grow experiences

When your child experiences something for the first time, pay attention. Avoid judgement about their response to it if they're reticent or uncertain. Avoid phrases like 'Don't be a baby/stupid/spoilsport'. Think, 'What do I want them to learn from this? Where is the positive I can make them feel good about? What is the most encouraging thing I can say?' Focus on praising qualities like determination more than the actual achievement.

For example, the other day I observed Tara, my daughter-in-law, with Heath when he was exploring a climbing frame for the first time. He was quite tentative. She avoided labelling that negatively. Instead she said, 'Are you taking it nice and carefully? That's a good idea until you get used to it. Good boy, no need to hurry, just go up one rope at a time if you can...that's right.' Everything he did, including choosing not to climb higher, was rewarded with a positive response, 'Is that high enough for now? That's fine. Well done for giving it a go.' There was no suggestion of failure, only achievement. And later that afternoon he was scampering all over it without a hint of worry.

When Philip Larkin wrote,

They fuck you up, your mum and dad

he was, to a large degree, talking about how these equivalences, and the misreading of cause and effect in situations, stack up over time and even across generations. Children who don't receive signals from their own parents that they're loved and valued often grow up into parents who either don't send those signals themselves, or who send messages that project their own sense of low self-esteem or helplessness onto their children. I remember one mother who came to see me who felt consistently let down by her father after her parents divorced. She would sit for hours in the window of her mum's house waiting for his car to pull up, and be disappointed more often than not. She realised, through reflecting on the causal effect of this experience, that her default response to any excitement in her children was, 'Don't get too excited, it probably won't happen'. Negative messages get passed down from generation to generation like unwanted heirlooms.

Plastic fantastic

Scientific research has proved beyond doubt that our brain is plastic. You only have to read of stroke victims whose brains have rewired themselves to work around damage in order to reconnect lost abilities to acknowledge this. It's my belief that this plasticity applies equally to our sense of self. **We are not stuck being us.** Our sense of self isn't a uniform, it's a character in a story your brain writes to guide us safely (if not always happily) through life. Once we realise this we can begin to become the writer of our story and turn it into an epic. Let's teach our children how to take control of their narrative from an early age.

CHAPTER 2:

Our culture's toxins

Mistaking acquisition for growth

We are living in the most affluent era of human history, and yet, in western culture, depression has become an epidemic. The World Health Organisation predicts that it will be the second most devastating disease by 2020. In Britain, according to the Office of National Statistics, 10% of the 60 million population is depressed at any one time. I think our consumer culture is to blame with its emphasis on the pursuit of 'stuff'. For the overwhelming majority of us adequate food and shelter is a given, which allows us the luxury of aspiration. Are we living up to the expectations we set for ourselves or had set for us? These are questions we have the luxury of contemplating. How do we know the answers? Usually by the symbols we've been sold as success badges such as houses, cars, clothes and labels. 'Stuff'. We've been seduced by the retail industry into believing that their products in some way represent to others who we are. How can we be seen in the best way by those around us? By collecting the same badges as them but a bit shinier. From the moment we are capable of reaching out with our hands we are subject to the attempts of others to influence our choices. Those attempts are becoming increasingly insidious and almost impossible to ignore or avoid. When companies harness our fragile young egos in pursuit of greater profits they can do great damage to our self-esteem and turn us into people who sacrifice happiness in a never-ending pursuit of status.

Advertising

There was a time when advertisements for products like shoes used to focus on the quality of their manufacture and how long they'd last. Now it's more about how cool you'll be for wearing them for the three months they survive before falling apart, just in time for the next season's colours. It's an exaggeration to say that one man was responsible for this change but not much of one. Edward Bernays became interested in the power of propaganda after working on Woodrow Wilson's campaign to shift American public opinion towards favouring intervention in First World War. He was amazed at how the public were able to be swayed and wondered whether such tactics could be employed during peacetime. Bernays invented the term Public Relations – yes, PR is his fault – and called his techniques of moulding opinion the *engineering of consent*. One success, for which we can all be grateful, is his work for the tobacco industry in making it socially acceptable for women to smoke in public. In 1929, Bernays staged the Easter Parade in New York City and had models pose with lit cigarettes as 'torches of freedom'. Increased frequency of lung cancer in women became a measure of their emancipation.

His ideas spread quickly. In 1952, two of Bernays' contemporaries were asked by the food company General Mills to help them promote their new invention – instant cake mix. Women just weren't buying it. Their solution was to remove the powdered egg from the mix so that the cook had to add one. The reasoning? It made women feel as if they were still cooks. Science has shown quite clearly that we're not really creatures of logic, that our emotions actually govern most of our decisions. This is one example. Logically, it makes no sense to increase the complexity of what is intended as a labour- and time-saving device but, emotionally, adding an egg and stirring the mixture gives us a greater sense of creating something. And in the 1950s, for many, a wife's self-worth was measured by her culinary dexterity. This was both Bernays' genius and his terrible legacy. He recognised that people could be induced to buy things to make them feel better about themselves. Unfortunately, for the reasons I've described thus far, none of us leave childhood with our self-worth entirely intact. Our brains search for ways to enhance it in the eyes of our loved ones and neighbours. That lurking feeling that we're not quite up to scratch compared to others leaves us as fruit ripe for the picking. The result has been the rise of a consumer culture fed by a retail therapy industry that promises us we'll feel 'worth it' if we wear their products. Sadly, it can also mean that we feel better parents if our kids are dressed in the current 'in' label, pushed in the 'right' pushchair, and met at the school gates in the 'best' car.

I had a client who came to see me with chronic stress. A potent symbol of what was stressing him was his inability to afford the latest model of the car he drove. His car was just a year old. 'What's the difference?', I asked. 'Well, the headlights are a different shape . . .' and then he tailed off. It became apparent that it wasn't about the car, it was about what he drove into the car park of the financial services company he worked for. Or, more accurately, what he had to park next to – the new cars of his young and thrusting colleagues. As has always been the case, his brain was comparing him to the rest of his tribe and calculating what it would take to get him nearest to the fire (or in his case the next desk up the career ladder). Our Neolithic heritage has left us with a mental scanner that calculates how we're doing in relation to those we view as belonging to our tribe – and in a global village that club has expanded massively.

This need we have to be seen as belonging to the tribe, and well thought of by its members, leaves us susceptible to being manipulated by people who cleverly see the opportunity to link their products to our emotional need to feel accepted by others.

If our childhood leaves us feeling that we are never

accepted as being quite good enough, we become a bottom-less pit of consumer spending. This often traps us in jobs we don't like doing in order to pay for things that don't make us feel as good as we think everybody else feels. That's the culture we were raised in and which we're raising our children in. One that prompts a protection response at every thought or suggestion that we might lose the symbols of our status. Where **we mistake acquisition for growth.**

It's why, as parents, focusing your child on 'success' through the typical definition of it is a recipe for a life of unfulfilled struggle. One of collecting badges that, once you get them home, never shine as brightly as the advertising promised.

It takes great courage on the part of modern parents to refuse to kit their children in what seem to be the favoured labels of the other mums at the school gate, to refuse to update their phones because their friends have the latest version, or to not hot-house them to get the 'best start' in life. But from what I see in my clinic, if you raise your child to value people and nature more than material possessions, to pursue the fun of challenging themselves in whatever they find interesting, and avoid pushing them into *your* version of *their* best life, in time you'll actually be able to sit back and enjoy watching what they make of their life without a therapist on speed dial.

Parenting Tip: Nature will nurture the best of your child

This is going to take bravery. Limit your child's access to advertising wherever possible – avoid live TV, for example. There is a movement called 'Rewild the Child'. Check it out. The more you get your children in touch with nature, the less they'll be swayed by what advertisers want them to care about.

And if our society's petri dish didn't have enough toxins in it from the advertising industry, we still have the media to top it up . . .

Don't read all about it

My grandmother was part of a remarkable generation. Born in 1915, she was alive when planes were just making an appearance and was still alive when we reached the moon. She lived her whole life in a ten-mile radius but heard stories from her children and grandchildren about the places they lived in or visited all across the world. She went from being told what was happening in the world by her father reading from his newspaper to hearing about it almost instantly on a 24-hour news channel.

If we went back to her grandmother, the picture would be one where the pace of news was even slower. Before the invention of the telegraph in the 1830s news travelled at the speed of the fastest horse, pigeon or ship. The Battle of Trafalgar was fought off the coast of Spain on 21 October

1805. News of it reached the London public on 6 November. The fall of the Alamo in Texas on 6 March 1836 was reported in *The Times* in London on 17 May. The great advantage of such a limited news system was that people were exposed to less bad news. This was very good news – for them.

Research shows that our minds are sensitised towards paying particular attention to bad news. A study by psychologists at the University of Zurich found that when people were given reports on a health risk, they found the research more credible when it highlighted a risk than when it found no danger. We believe things more when we're told something is wrong than when we're told there's evidence the situation is OK. If we look to our ancestors for the reason, it makes sense. Our brains are looking for potential threats because in the old days so many threats could kill us. In any situation the first question our unconscious must answer is, 'Am I vulnerable?' Hearing that your neighbour drowned by falling off a particular cliff warns you to be careful. Hearing that a neighbour didn't fall off a cliff probably isn't a story to keep you spellbound around the camp fire.

Seen in that light, the dreadful focus of the media on all things negative begins to make sense. I used to believe it was all part of a government conspiracy – if the focus is kept on the threats in the world, we're more likely to keep needing to feel protected by our rulers. While I still have a lurking suspicion there's something in that, I'm not so sure it's the key reason. Daniel Gardner in *The Science of Fear* opened my eyes to the possibility that it's just the result of reporters being human too. They write what people like to read about because they like it themselves. When they're scanning for possible headlines it's the bad ones their brains pick up first.

What began as an adaptive benefit has now become a drawback. In a world where the bad news we were aware of was limited to the small number of people in our lives and the small area of the world we were privy to, the negatives that arrived every day were manageable and useful. Now, with the 24-hour news cycle and the internet, we're surrounded by bad news all the time, from all around the world. In recent days while writing this I've been bombarded by images of Hurricane Sandy hitting New York; a major electrical retailer in the UK going bankrupt; the potential wiping-out of Britain's ash trees; Jimmy Savile's appalling perversion, and Chelsea losing to Manchester United. What is my brain supposed to do with such a relentless tide of negatives? Go into ancestral habits most likely and start releasing adrenaline to get me ready to run, fight or freeze. The favoured word for this is stress, a lower level of threat preparedness than a full-on panic attack, but one familiar to most of us. The trouble is, adrenaline was only supposed to be a chemical for emergencies. It was intended to propel us away from danger (or kill its source) after which we could take the rest of the day off and have a snooze somewhere safe. Nowadays, we probably see more mayhem on TV while we're eating our breakfast than cavemen witnessed in a year. Adrenalin is quite toxic over the long term. This low-level release of it in response to the news, with the fears it triggers for our own and our family's security, means that our immune system can get depleted trying to flush it out of our bodies, thus opening us up to various illnesses and diseases – including depression.

This exposure to bad news tunes the brain to believe we live in a world of threat and are in need of being in a state of protection. It kills our natural urge towards growth. Turning off the news and cancelling the papers is a good first step on the road to recovery.

Watching the news or reading newspapers reduces our ability to think for ourselves because we get subtly indoctrinated into the worldview of the media magnates. They get to pick what we see and read. It also introduces cognitive errors into our thinking by wrapping things into simplistic sound bites that are seductive but usually madly simplistic: x causes banking crisis, y to blame for z disaster. Avoid the news and keep your children away from it too. Making the news a regular part of your day is like keeping a sabre-tooth tiger as a pet.

Parenting Tip: Show them a world of growth not protection

Cherry pick what you want your child to see happening in the world. This isn't denial, it's minimising their exposure to things they have no control over. Highlight positive stories that demonstrate people succeeding against the odds, being compassionate, being brave, seeking new horizons. Watch with them and make these subjects conversation pieces on the school run.

And then there's what we choose for entertainment . . .

Soaps that don't wash clean

The TV soaps of my childhood were gentle things. For a long time, watching *Coronation Street* was like stepping into a pair of comfy slippers of an evening, seeing largely everyday troubles get resolved within a few episodes by the pulling together of the community. I doubt anybody under thirty would equate my description with the 'Corrie' they know now. Over the last twenty-five years, British soaps have become the prime nurturer of the idea that he who shouts loudest wins, that everything has to be a drama and that what you want always trumps what anybody else needs.

I think life in Britain is increasingly reflecting that 'art'. Collectively, we create the world as a version of *EastEnders*. Collectively, our reality becomes *Big Brother*. The celebration of dysfunction is widespread. Celebrity without talent, effort or point has become an aspirational career for many young people. It's the tinniest of badges. The trouble is, it's promoting protection. It's adding to the adrenaline burden we place on our bodies. To encourage our children to seek conflict, and celebrate division and unkindness, not only sets them up for an increased likelihood of anxiety and depression in adulthood, it also tunes their brain to interpret the world in this way.

When it comes to reality television, it's rare for it to focus on anything aspirational. *Big Brother* tends to be a collection of grotesques looking for attention. Viewers are invited to celebrate victimhood rather than resilience. X

Factor seduces the young into thinking that celebrity is a career option where talent isn't a necessary prerequisite. Television is not a healthy habit.

Parenting Tip: Think before you watch

You know what I'm going to say, avoid soaps. Avoid 'reality' TV. Do show them people struggling against challenges, but programmes that focus on the strength of the struggler, not the drama they can wallow in. Show people working hard for what they have, not expecting success as a right. Teach them what it takes to be great at something.

The story so far

Our species journey has taken us from a single cell in a petri dish, to someone who looks in a mirror and likes what they see – or doesn't – simply as a result of what they believe about what has happened to them, and often because of how many of our society's symbols of success we've managed to accumulate. We live trapped in the reality that our brain creates without us realising it.

Now you do realise, we can begin to do something to make *you* the creator of yourself, and, in turn, teach your children to do the same.

PART II:
GROWING A BETTER 'YOU'

Now that I've outlined how we become the way we are, I'm going to give you some tools to change it. I'm not suggesting change is easy, but it is possible. I'd rather have you in front of me in my clinic but that would make things a bit crowded, so, in the absence of being able to do therapy directly with you, I'm going to help you do your own.

I've divided what I want to teach you into three lessons. As we go through I've included some questions to ask yourself in situations where you feel stressed or challenged. My hope would be that these become so familiar to you that they become a habit of mind, a reflexive response to a situation. That will take practice. I've also included some exercises called 'Work the Problem'. I've found them tremendously helpful in avoiding running round like a headless chicken instead of solving an issue. You'll get from them what you put in. Please don't just read them and think magic will happen. Nothing will happen unless you make it happen. Which, actually, is the heart of my first lesson.

Be ILOC

You have power over your mind – not outside events. Realise this and you will find strength

Marcus Aurelius

I spent a lot of my life waiting to be discovered. Something told me that I was destined for great things, so it didn't really matter what I was currently doing. At some point the world would realise what it was missing and elevate me to my true position. No wonder King Arthur was my favourite story as a boy, and *The Matrix* my favourite film as a man. I was expecting Merlin or Morpheus to show up. They never did.

This is what is known as having an External Locus of Control (ELOC). It's when we think our lives are shaped by things outside of us, that the world has the power to 'make us' feel things. This belief influences us in any number of ways, both large and small. How many people dream of what they'd do if they won the lottery? Or of how their life would be different if only they weren't held back by their upbringing, their partner, their family, or just their plain bad luck? How many of you have sat and hoped for something to happen to improve your situation, or even negotiated with your God or the universe that if things went a particular way you'd do something in return, that's all ELOC, my friend.

Waiting for the cavalry to come over the hill will usually end up with you being scalped by life.

ILOC is the big goal of this book. It stands for Internal Locus of Control and is a mindset where the holder takes responsibility for what happens. It's the difference between somebody saying, 'Something should be done' and someone saying 'I'm going to do it'. Someone operating from ILOC can't have a bad day because of the actions of others or as a result of what the world throws at them. Not because their boss shouting at them, or their partner leaving, won't have an effect on them but because they choose what that effect is going to be. An ILOC mindset puts you back in the driving seat. **Nobody can take your power, you can only give it away.**

Society tends to breed an ELOC perspective. It makes us look outside of ourselves for solutions to things – usually at a price. Since the Second World War there has been a gradual shift from the independence and resilience of our ancestors to the 'from-cradle-to-grave welfare' expectations of our society and the 'buy my product to like yourself more' hogwash that fuels our rampant consumerism.

How to develop ILOC

Knowing is not enough, we must apply. Willing is not enough,
we must DO   **Bruce Lee**

Imagine you were climbing in the high Andes with your
friend and broke your leg. While lowering you down a cliff,
your friend was forced to cut the rope and let you fall in
order to save his own life. Rather than die you fell down a
bottomless crevasse which you had no chance of climbing
out of. What would you do? You're lying on a narrow ledge.
No help is coming. You can't climb up because of your leg.
I suspect many of us would still scream for help anyway
and then, eventually, die. Joe Simpson was in exactly this
position. He climbed down. Deeper into a crevice he couldn't
see the bottom of, deeper into the dark. He went in the only
direction available for him. Not because there was a chance
of escape that way, simply because it was the only choice
involving action open to him. That is ILOC. In this case,
fortune favoured the deserving. It did lead to the way out.
From there he only had to bum-shuffle five miles with no
food and little water. It took him three days. He arrived at
base camp just before his friend packed up. *That* is resilience.

Focus on results

Many people come to see me with the vaguely defined but
very clear feeling that they're 'stuck'. As a label for what ails

them it's surprisingly common. When their story unfolds, they're usually repeating a cycle of doing more of what isn't working for them. Einstein said the definition of insanity is doing the same thing over and over again and expecting a different result. I see it in people who repeatedly experience bad relationships or jobs that are a cul-de-sac or end in the same frustration or lack of fulfilment. Even though we aren't happy with what we have, we can often find ourselves stuck, creating all the reasons why we can't do anything about it. I make a point of separating *reasons* from *results*.

When someone tells you about a goal they have they'll usually be full of enthusiasm for it at the beginning. Catch up with them a while later and ask them how it's going and you'll get one of two responses: they'll either give you a result – that they've reached their goal or are concretely closer, or they'll give you all the reasons why they haven't been able to do so. **Results versus reasons.** Often those reasons are many and convincing. Life will always throw obstacles in the way of success. It's how you respond to obstacles that makes the difference. If you read the obituaries of successful people what you get is a list of their results. What you don't read is, 'If only her children hadn't held her back/if his family had been more supportive/if the economy had been kinder/if she hadn't waited so long . . . he/she'd have changed the world'.

Either a result, or a list of reasons why you didn't get to where you were aiming, is at the end of any journey that involves a goal. Which will be your fate is largely in your hands. One of the biggest lessons I've ever learned is to **Take Action.** It's my mantra, and the thing that I attribute more to the change in my life (and personality) over the last fifteen years than anything else.

Taking action is the mantra that will keep you moving

In any situation where you have a choice or where life is throwing you a curve ball, if you learn to ask yourself, 'What is it I can do here?' it opens up the possibility of action. **There is nearly always something you can do. Anything more than nothing is something.**

> **Self-question 1: What is it I can do here?**

You've probably come across the Serenity prayer:

Grant me the serenity to accept the things I cannot change;
Courage to change the things I can;
And the wisdom to know the difference.

I love the sentiment, other than 'Grant me'. That's ELOC. I'd prefer a version that's a mantra, not a prayer:

Accept the things I cannot change;
Develop the courage to change the things I can;
And have the wisdom to know the difference.

Not as serene, I grant you, but more in keeping with my point.

Think of your life as having two circles:

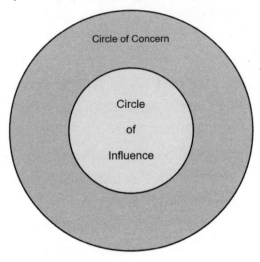

The circle of influence contains the things you can do something about. The circle of concern is full of the things that bother you that you can't directly influence. We can waste a lot of time and thought bouncing around in the circle of concern. It tends to increase our anxiety levels. Train yourself to take action about the things within your circle of influence. Let go of the things in your circle of concern. This will massively increase your ability to stay centred. Whenever you're feeling overwhelmed by life, or you face a particular challenge, draw these circles out and write in them the things that are on your mind. See where each challenge, concern or worry belongs. Then do what you can about whatever is in your influence. Accept those things you can't have an effect on. Leave them behind.

For example, in my circle of concern I could put global warming. Thinking about the scale of the problem, and its future impact on my family's life, can become quite over-whelming. What can I do about it? In my circle of influence, I can put my commitment to recycle, to reduce my carbon footprint, to live sustainably. If I want to do more I could expand that circle by joining Greenpeace and by campaigning on environmental issues. I could expand it further by going into politics. I could, conceivably, become Prime Minister. It's for us to choose the extent of our influence and the time and effort we want to put into maximising it.

Another example might be your children's education. In your circle of concern you might put the over-emphasis on testing not suiting your child, the right school not being available, and the cost of university education for them when they're older. The list of what concerns you about your chil-dren's future is probably nearly limitless once you get started. So what can you put in your circle of influence? How about what you can teach them about what you consider important? Can you increase the time you give your children and spend it on learning? Could you become a school governor? Could you homeschool? Could you save anything towards their degree? All of you will have different degrees of wiggle room in answer to these questions. That's fine. The key point is to be in charge of what you decide can be done.

This is the heart of ILOC. If a thing can be done by you, do it. If it can't, but it can be done by someone else, get them to do it. If nobody can do anything about it, accept it, let it go, and move on. All three are actions you're taking, rather than passively hoping someone else will do the solving for you.

As His Holiness the Dalai Lama wisely pointed out, 'If it can be solved, there's no need to worry, and if it can't be solved, worry is of no use.'

When the going gets tough...

The purpose of self-development isn't to smooth the seas of life. It's to make you better able to cope with the waves, because not only are big waves inevitable, they're often necessary for growth.

Imagine something going wrong in your day, something 'bad' by your reckoning. Maybe think of a recent example. Ask yourself these questions:

Work the Problem

- How is this about the situation and not about you?
- Is how I'm interpreting this situation true?
- Is a bad interpretation the only possible one?
- If this was happening to someone else, would it automatically mean the same thing to them?
- What do I fear other people could think about me because of this situation?
- Why doesn't that actually have to be true?
- What could I gain from this?
- If this had to happen for me to learn something vital from it, what would it be?

What I want you to do is get better at differentiating those events that would (and should) knock people for six, such as the loss of a loved one, from those life challenges where the response to them is less universal. For example, redundancy. I've had clients who arrive depressed at the prospect, and those who are bouncing with excitement. Sometimes one becomes the other in the space of a single session. Questions like, 'Where's the opportunity here?' and my core ILOC question, 'What can **I** do **here, now?**' help you to keep your mind open to other possibilities of meaning. As does a mantra my wife and I use to remind us to stop flapping and get solving – 'Work the Problem'. Keep your mind on the search for solutions, don't let it keep marinating in the problem.

This is something you are going to fail at remembering to do, regularly. Good. We're only human. There are going to be times when a situation overwhelms you and you default to ELOC. It just makes it another situation to learn from to get you better at staying ILOC.

Fail, learn, forgive, reset. Begin again.

No failure, only feedback, kind of...

What would you do differently in your life if you weren't scared you'd fail? Our relationship to failure often defines what we achieve. It's vital to get that relationship right if you want to develop the skill of living the ILOC way.

It's irritating when people say failure is not an option.

What rubbish. Failure is always an option, in fact it's usually the easiest option. It's also a key ingredient for growth. Bruce Lee said, 'The man who never made a mistake never made anything'. The same goes for failures. **You learn the most at the edge of what you are capable of, so failure is part of the deal for anyone looking to grow.**

Why have I called this section **no failure, only feedback?** Glad you asked. This is one of those phrases that gets almost chanted at you on NLP training sessions, and I subscribe to it, with some caveats. It's not what happens to you, it's what you make of it. Fail, fail often, fail spectacularly, but don't use failures to diminish yourself. Learn from them. Many of my clients come to see me crushed by life, feeling they've failed, fearing they will fail again. They are stuck in an unfulfilled life (often the very life they feared) because of how scared they are of what they make failure mean about them: that they are a loser, that their failure was intrinsically caused by something wrong with them rather than retrievable errors or the force of circumstances. I remind them that Abraham Lincoln lost eight elections and failed in two businesses. JK Rowling was once at a place in her life where she described herself as 'the biggest failure she knew'. My job is to help my clients see failure differently. To see it as a necessary step along the road of growth, as a place to learn and become stronger. **There is no winning or losing. Just winning and learning.**

So it is with your children. Watching them fail, and being with them through the aftermath, is one of the most painful things for a parent to endure. Every part of you screams to do something about it to make it better. You can't, it's miserable, and necessary. What you can do is make it useful.

The most creative people have a tolerance for failure, the most creative companies encourage it. The Pixar mindset is, 'Screw up as quickly as possible. Find the fault so you can get to the fix quicker'. **Fearing failure stunts your growth,** being curious about failure takes you beyond your current thinking and allows you to explore new possibilities.

Failure is just the universe saying, 'That way didn't work'. It's not a verdict about you as a person. That's key with your children and the explanatory style you adopt with them. For example, the failure might be about something to do with the environment the failure occurred within.

On the course in Cognitive Hypnotherapy we have run for many years, at graduation, we used to teach people how to break a one-inch-thick pine board with their bare hand. It looks impossible but it's actually very straightforward if you follow the steps. One day after a graduation my son Stuart, who was about seventeen at the time, spotted me unloading some left-over pine boards from the car and asked if he could break one. We set up the concrete blocks the board sits on, on the decking in the garden. Stuart performed the action with perfect form, he'd done it successfully loads of times since he was about ten, but this time the board didn't break. That stings. He tried again. It still didn't break. He marched off full of injured teenage pride – i.e. he made it a personal failure; somehow he'd lost his mojo.

I stepped up and had a go. It didn't break either. I was

puzzled. I've broken hundreds. I got curious about my failure. If it's not about me, what else could it be about? I swapped boards in case it was a tough one. Still failed. Curious-er and curious-er. Then I had a light bulb moment and moved the blocks onto the path. The board broke easily. So did the next. Stu came back and broke his first time. The failure hadn't been anything to do with Stuart as a person, the springiness of the deck was absorbing the force of the impact. It was an issue of environment.

Address failure by answering the following question, and then complete the following three steps:

> **Self-question 2: How is this not about me as a person?**

Step 1: Was there something about where the failure occurred that was a factor?

What Stuart succumbed to was a thing in psychology called *attribution error*: we tend to overestimate the impact a person has on a situation and underestimate the impact of their surroundings. In a classic experiment, a group of volunteers were invited to watch two teams of players shooting hoops at either end of a basketball court and vote on which team was best. Overwhelmingly the group voted for team 'A'. The volunteers were replaced and the experiment was run again. Again the group voted for team 'A'. Which was strange, because team 'A' and team 'B' had swapped ends while the volunteers were being replaced. What was actually behind their choice? The lighting at the end of the most successful team was brighter than the other end. Both 'better' teams could just see the hoop better but neither group of spectators had factored this into their decision. They'd attributed the greater accuracy purely to the talent of the individuals.

Step 2: Look at your actions (not you, but your actions, that distinction is important). Were they part of the failure?
- What did you do that worked?
- What did you do that didn't?
- What did you do that you'd do differently?
- What didn't you do that you could or should have?

Step 3: Look at skills and capabilities:
- Where did your skills match the challenge – i.e. where were you good enough?
- Where are your current skills lacking?
- What can you do to improve them?
- What traits or capabilities (like determination, creativity, enthusiasm etc.) did you bring?
- What traits or capabilities would have helped you?
- How can you develop them?
- Who has them that you could learn from?

Through this three-step process you can nudge towards a belief about the failure that isn't pessimistic – i.e. isn't *personal* (it's not about me), *pervasive* (it's just about this one situation, not everything I do), or *permanent* (it won't always be like this), and develop a plan to move forward with something that will make it, with hindsight, a springboard to something better. The repeated experience of this mindset changes the prospect of failure and, in doing so, makes it less likely. Not that failure will happen less often, only that you won't identify it that way so frequently.

Success is a habit

We are what we repeatedly do. Excellence, then, is not an act, but a habit.

Aristotle

We are a bundle of habits. Every day we are engaged in scores of behaviours that we give no thought to. From brushing our teeth or putting a pair of trousers on, to driving a car or having a favourite time for a cup of coffee, we hand over an awful lot of our day to our unconscious. In the main that helps us, but often we don't realise that some of the things we don't like about our lives are also caused by habitual patterns of behaviour, including our responses to food, criticism, exercise, or the way we do our jobs. So many people walk around hypnotised by their habits – I often see my job as a Cognitive Hypnotherapist as a 'de-hypnotist', helping people take back control of situations where their habits take over.

It's easy to underestimate their power until you think of habits this way:

Success is a series of actions, repeated.
Failure is a series of actions, repeated.

Both are created the same way.

The key to living more happily is to create the habits that take you towards what you want, because **we become what we do most of.** The more you behave as a person who is ILOC, the more your brain will interpret the world around you through that filter and make your reality one where you're surrounded by the possibilities for positive action. You become the kind of person who lives in that kind of world.

So the task I'm setting you is to think of a number of small changes in your behaviour which, if you did them every day, would help you grow in the direction you'd like to. Making them small is important. People are always looking for big, dramatic transformations, but change is much more likely through building permanent momentum through small nudges.

For example:

- I've committed to doing ten minutes exercise every day. That's not a lot but I find that if I do ten then, more often than not, I end up doing more. But on days when the idea of running six miles would put me off, the thought of just running for ten minutes makes putting my trainers on bearable.
- I've committed to reading ten pages of something uplifting every day. It's easy to find and better than newspapers. It also gives me new ideas.

- I've committed to eating my five a day – as you'll read later, I've not been the world's best user of vegetables.

As a parent you could:

- Commit to spending ten minutes a day focused on what your child wants to do.
- Spend ten minutes on something just for you, cut off from everything.
- Put aside some time to spend planning a family project, with everyone involved. Give everyone a task.
- Do a physical activity with your children every day, if only for ten minutes. Watching them doesn't count.
- Find something to discuss as a family. Task your children to find something they'd like to talk about. Everyone gets the chance to talk to everyone about what interests them.

They're small things that are easy to do and just as easy to leave out or overlook. But if you write them down, and make the crossing out of them a standard part of your day, you'll find that your attitude changes. You feel more in control of the choices you're making. A strange cascade effect takes place where being in control of particular choices like this becomes a way of being in more and more control of your life. They're a symbol of an attitude that will pervade your character because remember, the more something happens, the more it will happen. This is true of the habits that hold us back and is just as true of the habits that move us forward. We're just tuning our brain to the frequency for growth and making ILOC itself a habit.

Here's a top tip: if you tie a new habit to a current behaviour – like always reading the ten pages when you're sitting with your morning coffee – you're more likely to do it.

Parenting Tip: Get them in the habit

Ask yourself, what small habits could you get your children to adopt that would build the ILOC mentality? Small things that are easy to do and which build to a longer-term benefit that's important to them? Think of small things they become responsible for, like practising a skill or contributing towards a trip or holiday. For example, if it's football, what are three small things they could do each day that would specifically build their skill – not just 'play football for ten minutes'.

Feed what you focus on

One of the daily habits I want you to start is to spend a few minutes each day focusing on your good points. Keep a journal beside the bed and review your day. Write down everything you did that you're proud of – not 'I split the atom today' pride, necessarily (but go you (!) if you did), but any moment where you recognised you were ILOC, where you demonstrated a positive trait or characteristic. Where you stood up for something, where you performed an act of kindness, where you did something well. **We feed what we focus on,** so focusing on your positives will not only make them stronger, they'll become a more prevalent part of your day. A lot of who we think we are is taken from what we find ourselves doing, so shining a spotlight on your strengths will increase your self-esteem. In just a few minutes a night, you can really boost your belief in yourself and what you can achieve. To help you with this I've developed a download for you to listen to after writing your good points down. It will prime your mind to go searching for more examples to create your reality with. It's at www.questinstitute.co.uk/growdownloads

Who decides who you are?

This tricksy notion of identity is central to the problem of retaining control of our choices. Does my identity control my attitude to things or does something else? Psychology has demonstrated that both our environment and the actions of people around us influence the way we behave and our sense of ourselves. What this means is that, rather than having a singular sense of who we are – as in 'take me as you find me' – it's really more a case of 'take me where you find me, or with whom you find me'. How many of you will admit that you can be a very different person around your family compared to your friends or at work compared to at home? All of us have a sense of self that is more fluid than that self allows us to believe. This leaves us vulnerable to outside influence because situational triggers can cause a lesser version of you to suddenly hijack your behaviour. It used to be the case that just my wife asking me to put a shelf up would turn me into a nervous wreck because my dad was never the most patient of teachers and would quickly mock my attempts at DIY. At those moments, the person I presented as 'me' was a world away from the person you'd generally meet who I'd consider to be 'myself'.

On the positive side, studies show that if important people show belief in us we tend to raise our performance to fit their expectations. Surrounding ourselves with positive people will make us feel that we're a positive person. Joining a group committed to exercise can transform our attitude to exercise. Our environment can be far more important to how we feel about ourselves than we often realise. I've read that **we're a composite of the five people we spend most time with.** Think about that. Are your five good influences?

It means we can be influenced to lower our performance by a manager who takes against us, we can lose our self-confidence under the dripping-tap influence of an unsupportive partner, and we can become fatter by hanging out with overweight friends. The difference I perceive in myself from when I was surrounded by the police culture (and nature of the work) to now, being surrounded by an amazing network of positively inclined therapists (and nature of the work), is huge. While my *self* will attribute much of the credit to *itself*, in truth, my surroundings provided much of the impetus.

> **Task:**
>
> Conduct an audit of the 5 people you spend most time with, or are most influenced by.
> - Are they contributing to growth or unnecessary protection?
> - Are they helping you move forward or holding you back?

Sometimes we hang onto friends simply out of loyalty or nostalgia, even when they're no longer on the same page as us. That happened a lot when I left the police. In the end, I let go of a lot of people I valued because they just didn't support the direction I wanted to point my life in and I found it a drain to push against their energy. Don't be afraid of letting people go. If you're in growth, there'll be plenty of new people to connect to who feed your aspirations.

If you are working to become ILOC, and pursue a life of growth, you'll find yourself at odds with a lot of society. Many people, including your friends, are likely to feel threatened by you striking away from the safe shores of 'normality'. They may respond negatively towards you. A question I find incredibly helpful in helping me to remain in growth under the assault of other people's criticism or negativity is this:

> **Self-question 3: What is it about them that makes them need to make me feel bad?**

The more you ask that question about them the more you'll see the limitations, weaknesses and fears that drive their behaviour. It makes it easier to ignore, and also easier to forgive. They're just a fellow struggler. Your behaviour is causing them to notice their struggle more than they want to. I was amazed after I left the police how many ex-colleagues asked how I was doing and seemed quietly disappointed that I was making a success of it. I now understand why. They were unhappy in the police too, they just didn't feel capable of doing what I had done, and felt bad about themselves as a result. My failure would have unconsciously comforted them, lovely people though they were.

The answer isn't out there

For a very long time we've been encouraged to surrender our control to experts. Feeling ill? See a doctor. Got a problem with a neighbour? Call the council or the police. Want to lose weight? There's an expert telling you about their new diet on every daytime TV programme. If you're prepared to pay, there's someone who will solve every problem you can possibly experience – and in the process cause you to forget to ask, 'What can I do about it myself?'

I see so many clients who are suffering from stress, anxiety or depression (or a combination of all three). When you get to the reason why, it's because of the pressure they feel to maintain the lifestyle 'people' expect of them. In his excellent book *Affluenza*, Oliver James writes:

Possession overload is the kind of problem where you have so many things you find your life is being taken up by maintaining and caring for things instead of people.

Often the two get confused. I've seen too many career-oriented people, mainly men, who were working hard to 'give their family everything', only to return to the luxury home one evening to find their family gone because they'd deprived them of the one thing they wanted most – their time.

We're encouraged to believe that retail is therapy, yet really owning 'stuff' can become a tyranny – it ends up owning you. It doesn't give you what you acquire it for. If you have an empty space inside you where your self-esteem should be, no amount of labels, body spray, flash cars or gorging on food is going to fill it. You have the power to change it from within rather than puff it up temporarily with this month's 'must have' item.

Task:

Look at how much of your life you're giving to maintaining the badges you've accumulated. So many people are working long hours to pay for things they don't have the time to enjoy. Becoming more ILOC can quickly become an exercise in asking, 'Do I need this?' 'Will that make me happier?' 'Do I want to live this way?' Your life may become very different.

Deal with life as it is, not how it's supposed to be

Our brains spend a great deal of time and energy on anticipating our future. It can be why, when things don't go the way it predicted, we continue to blunder along in denial of the situation we're in. We continue to deal with life as we'd like it to be, not as it actually is. You only have to look at the weeks of denial after the Brexit vote, and the call for a second referendum, to see this limitation in action.

Often, if we stay stuck in unnecessary protection for too long, our brains grow to prefer the predictability of our unhappiness stretching ahead of us, rather than the unpredictability of being better. Our brains like habits – and **our whole life can become a habit of unfulfillment that we struggle to break.** ILOC enables you to change that habit, adapt to what is going on around you, and use it to create a better future.

A neuroscientist called Reid Montague made the point that we run on batteries – we only have a finite supply of energy. Now, in the main, keeping us supplied doesn't take much thought. In fact, in the western world our rapidly growing problem is keeping our personal energy supply from flowing over the tops of our trousers. But, for the vast majority of our species' time on the planet, finding enough food to survive has been the major occupation of every day. Some argue the major focus of our evolution has been finding better and better ways of making sure we get fed. Our big brain may be the result of that pursuit.

Being able to see ourselves in the future turns our brains into prediction machines – so we can begin to plan for famine, think through alternative hunting methods, and calculate their likely success. Being able to see into the future has been a big success, but it comes with drawbacks.

We can spend quite a lot of now thinking about later, especially if we're bored, unhappy or stuck, and that's not necessarily productive. I had a client who admitted that the only thing that got him out of bed in the morning was the hope he'd win the lottery. He spent a lot of time each day dreaming what he'd do with the cash. Now, within limits, having a good daydream about something that's unlikely to happen is harmless and can probably even reduce stress if you're picturing yourself on a tropical paradise surrounded by the scantily clad objects of your particular fantasy. But some clients I've seen spend so much time drifting into these futures that they lose touch with the present.

In any situation you see as a problem or a setback ask yourself:

> **Self-question 4: What can I do here, now? Where is the opportunity here?**

The skill I want to help you cultivate through adopting an ILOC mentality is to be more aware of what is actually happening in the moment, not what your brain is trying to reflexively make of it, and choose your actions accordingly. See life as it is in that moment, not the disaster your brain is making it out to be nor how you'd like it to be, then take action. 'It is what it is' is a popular maxim. Yes, it is what it is. Now, what is the best you can make out of it? Where's the opportunity, what are your choices, what can you do here, now? Work the Problem.

Work the Problem

If a situation is stressing you, use the following to guide you:

- Write down all the fears you have about what might happen.
- Go through each fear and prepare a plan for what you could do if they came true.
- Scale the likelihood of each thing happening 1–10.
- Go through each one and work out actions that would reduce the score you've given.
- Write down all the possible positives that could arise from this situation.
- Go through each one and prepare a plan that would make those positives more likely to happen.
- Create some small behaviours you could do each day that, by following them, would most likely lead to the outcome(s) you'd like most.

ILOC-ution lessons

What I've found is that the journey people take with me in the therapy room is largely one between the starting point of ELOC and the destination of ILOC. Many clients begin by believing in my ability to change them. Notice that's ELOC. I can't change anybody. The people I'm successful with realise this and engage in the process – it becomes a collaboration; it's moved from *me* changing them to *us* changing them. The final step towards 'esteem independence' is when they realise they're doing all the heavy lifting in the relationship and they no longer need me. THAT, my friend, is therapy success, when you make yourself redundant because the client realises they have everything they need within themselves to be who they want. It was only the miscalculations of a youthful brain in the presence of negative (or negatively interpreted) events that set them going in the direction of protection instead of growth in the first place.

So, the key to becoming more ILOC is becoming aware of those things that grow your self-esteem – and feeding them at every opportunity, taking action rather than waiting for something to happen, and inoculating yourself against negative influences. By becoming that kind of person, you become a parent who can create the best possible petri dish for your children to thrive in.

The next thing I'm going to teach you is to stop taking the truth so seriously.

You can believe
what suits you best

What the Thinker thinks, the Prover proves

It can be very easy to see what we want, hope or expect to see. And it's just as easy to not see what doesn't fit with our world view. Have you ever been involved in a serious disagreement with someone about something in which you believed passionately? Of course you have. Did it amaze you that no matter what evidence you marshalled to destroy their argument they continued to hold on to their point of view? Were they equally amazed at you doing the same? When Margaret Thatcher died some people mourned her deeply, but others had a street party and stamped on her portrait.

Back in 1877, when Giovanni Schiaparelli observed a network of straight lines on Mars, it led to an explosion of public excitement, and the discovery of many more of these 'canals' by other observers. We now know (unless you believe the moon landings were faked) that it's actually an optical illusion caused by the brain's liking for connecting points (like mountains on a distant planet) to make lines.

If you're a climate change sceptic, chances are the fact that 97% of climate scientists disagree with you won't sway you. If you're a creationist, then human bones older than the Bible's age for the world will be ignored or denigrated. That's worrying enough, but what we believe about ourselves can be just as resistant to contrary evidence.

Orr's Law

Many years ago, I came across a model described by Dr Leonard Orr, which explains why this happens. Imagine your mind has two parts, the Thinker and the Prover. The adage is, '**What the Thinker thinks, the Prover proves.**' If your Thinker thinks you are a good person your Prover will filter and interpret everything that happens to you, or around you, to sustain that belief. But, likewise, if your Thinker thinks you're rubbish, guess what your Prover will do? It's why you sometimes hear people being given a compliment or positive feedback respond with, 'You're only saying that to be nice', or 'That only went well because . . .' and give you a reason external to themselves. It's a self-perpetuating system that reinforces the beliefs you hold the longer you hold them. It's a way of describing how we end up in a default position in life of growth or protection.

At the heart of this model lie beliefs – they're essentially *what* the Thinker thinks from. I'm bombarded with them in my therapy room on a daily basis, 'Life's against me', 'I don't deserve good things', 'I'm to blame (for everything)', 'Nobody loves me', 'I'll never be happy/slim/successful'. The theme is finite but the variations are many, and if I give clients the room, their Prover will furnish me with a long list of examples to 'prove' the belief is valid, completely unaware that they're locked in a Thinker/Prover feedback loop.

In most cases, the limiting belief (or beliefs) the client brings to therapy is the keystone; change that and all the symptomatic behaviour it generates will change as well. However, achieving this can be tricky because of the illusion that **what feels real feels true.** Let me explain.

The definition of a belief is 'an acceptance that something exists or is true, especially without proof'. Beliefs are running in the background throughout our day to enable us to make it through it. Think back to when you got up this morning and swung your legs from the bed to the floor. Did you have any thought that it might not still be there? Of course not. As you walked to the bathroom, did you check with each footstep that the floor was still solid? You'd look pretty odd if you did, and imagine how slow it would make your day. As our experience of the world grows we build a set of beliefs to guide our actions – useful shortcuts and generalisations intended to keep us safe and save energy. Overwhelmingly they've proved themselves a good idea. We have beliefs about everything – in fact it's impossible not to. I remember a conversation once with someone over dinner who was deeply into post-modernism, and at one point they insisted, 'I don't believe in anything.' I couldn't resist, 'Do you really believe that?' I asked. Beliefs are unavoidable, and whether they're about trusting the flooring or not trusting yourself, they work the same way. They have to feel true to get you to respond to them, so they have to feel real, even the ones that aren't; that's their trick. My job is to get you to not take them too seriously.

> *The test of a first-rate intelligence is the ability to hold two opposing ideas in mind at the same time and still retain the ability to function.*
>
> **F. Scott Fitzgerald**

I don't believe in life after death, I think that when we're dead that's it. That's a belief, right? At the same time I talk in my head to my dead grandfather regularly – and he gives me some pretty good advice. For a long time, I wrestled with this incongruity because of the inconsistency, until the penny dropped. **Beliefs are just conveniences; they're there for guidance, not as articles of faith demanding blind obedience.** Ever since that penny dropped, I've used beliefs to make me happy and keep me growing. While I know I don't believe in life after death, clearly I get a benefit from talking to my granddad, so why not? For me the mistake would be to think that I have to believe in life after death in order to continue our conversations. I've found holding conflicting beliefs and choosing which one you'll have most benefit using at any particular time is a lot of fun, and gives you considerable freedom of thought – as confusing as it can be for your friends.

Beliefs are what your Thinker uses to define your world, and what your Prover slaves away to validate by organising the way you see things in a way that fits them. And 'slaves' is not an understatement. It's a sad software fault in all of us that our brains would rather keep an old belief and squeeze the world into a shape that keeps it true, than go to the trouble of updating that belief.

It is in the DNA of beliefs to feel as if they are 'the truth'. That's the only way they can get you to act. If you 'kind of' believed the floor was solid in your bedroom you'd proceed with continual caution. No wonder we defend them so strongly. Often, the ones we hold about ourselves we hold so strongly they strangle any prospect of growth in our lives.

You can become free of the beliefs that bind you and develop beliefs that will support you living in growth. It's not easy, but it is possible.

Listen for when you find yourself believing something strongly, and take a moment to ask yourself:

Self-question 5: What is my Thinker thinking?

> **Work the Problem:**
>
> - What is my Prover doing here?
> - What else might be true instead?
> - What would my Thinker have to think if it was?
> - How would that change things?
> - Why don't I want that to happen?
>
> Chances are that's going to bring some things up to think about.

Read things that are opposite to your beliefs. I've often found that reading something that goes against my world-view ends up by enriching it. I mentioned Gil Boyne earlier in the book. When I attended my first training session with him I did so because I believed the opposite of what he did, in just about every area of therapy. It changed my life because I had to admit that what he was doing worked, as was what I was doing! So neither what he believed was true (that therapy HAD to be done his way), nor what I believed (that my way of doing things was the only or correct way).

I like the advice from Paul Saffo, to have 'strong opinions, weakly held'. Commit to what you believe, but be prepared to let go of it the moment your belief is no longer useful or deserving of your commitment.

Parenting Tip: Stay flexible

It's easy for our brains to turn to concrete as we end up doing the things we've always done in the way we've always done them.

- Shake up your routines regularly. Take different routes to work. Try out new exercise routines. Dabble in new hobbies. Read people you disagree with. Watch films that aren't your 'thing'. Try new food.
- Apply this advice to your children. Make trying new things the norm. Reward the discomfort of stretching out of their comfort zone. The best chance of discovering their life's passion is by looking everywhere for it, not the same places repeatedly.
- Also, encourage your children to do old things new ways. Putting a different foot first in your trousers might only seem a small encourager of behavioural flexibility, but we all know what grows from acorns. The key purpose is to get them to avoid settling prematurely into fixed patterns. It's a key to being creative.

Flexible parents will grow open-minded, curious children. I don't think there's a better gift to bequeath them.

You can choose
who you want to be

Who would I be if I did this?

The plasticity of the brain means that you are someone your brain is making up. You can either leave it to chance as to who you end up believing yourself to be, or you can take control and start writing yourself as the character you'd want to be, in the story you'd have most fun living. Here's a discovery that I think will help you become more flexible about who you are and who you aren't, about what you can and cannot do. It's surprising where big lessons can come from, because this is about eating your greens. Well, me not eating mine, actually.

For most of my life, I've been at war with vegetables. Salad came in for a particular level of contempt. Despite a lifelong enjoyment of keeping fit, I spent little time thinking about keeping healthy through my food choices. What is probably just a lucky constitution allowed me to get away with it.

That's changed. In the supermarket recently, I stood

beside Bex looking at the salad display and said, 'What shall we get? They all look delicious.' And I wasn't joking. Here's how that change came about:

A friend had recommended a book by Tim Ferris called *The 4-Hour Body*. Most people would consider me reasonably slim, but my body fat is higher than you'd imagine. I'm what is called a TOFI: thin on the outside, fat on the inside. The book was about how to reduce body fat, not lose weight, and that interested me. So I decided to give it a go. It includes a number of hardcore things – like icy showers – but I thought I'd start off easy and just cut out the things he says contribute to fat gain. I could eat meat and vegetables (no fruit). You could see my problem.

Biting the bullet, I asked Bex to put any veg she chose on my plate and I promised to eat it without complaint. For the first few days I had a mantra: I was eating 'meat and medicine', and it got me through the strangeness of it. Then I became aware of an increasing dissonance in my head. If it had been a conversation it would have gone like this: 'This actually tastes ok.' 'No it doesn't, you don't like veg.' 'But, you know, actually, I am really quite enjoying the tastes and textures.' 'Shut up. You don't like veg.' 'I know I didn't but . . .' 'La la la . . . NOT LISTENING. You aren't someone who likes vegetables.'

And then a question sprung into my head:

Self-question 6: Who would I be if I...?

It was like being under the cold shower that Tim Ferris had encouraged me to take. In an instant, I realised that all these years it hadn't been about the vegetables themselves, it had been about 'Who would I be if I did like vegetables?'

Like a film on rewind, I recalled childhood images of the times I was made to stay at the table to finish my dinner when everyone else had gone. I can remember hiding things under a lip of the dinner table and putting loads of salad cream on my school plate so I could sink the salad beneath it out of the view of the shrewish dinner ladies. At home and at school, my childhood finicky nature with food was confronted and it became a war. Me against authority, with green things as the battleground. I don't remember ever losing. My whole life I've reacted strongly – including over-reacting – against anyone imposing their will on me, and lettuce was at the root of it.

'Who would I be if I was someone who ate vegetables and salad?' The answer my unconscious was using was clear: a weakling. Someone who surrenders. Someone who does as he's told. What a load of rubbish. I'd been a version of myself based on that?

'Who would I be if I was someone who liked green stuff?' Someone who felt instantly happier, more in control of their choices, and definitely healthier, that's who. How weird. I've realised that I've been carrying a stomach around inside me that's been unhappy with my diet for so long I'd forgotten it could feel any different. For the first time, it now feels like it belongs to me.

Who would I be if I...?

This question became a very important one. Bex and I started to use it when we confronted any limitation or reluctance to do something. 'I don't want to . . .' is met with 'Who would I be if I did want to?' and it's led to some interesting realisations, especially that a lot of things I 'don't want to do' I'm glad I did after I've done them.

I've talked about how we are the creators of ourselves. This food experiment gave me a chance to witness that fact, from the exposure of an unconscious belief to its instant updating when it was opened up to the light of the present day.

We have the opportunity to be who we want to be every time we wake up, and yet we tend to dress ourselves in our old beliefs each morning as inevitably as we put on our pants. We really don't have to.

There is probably no limit to what this simple question could accomplish – which is why many will ignore it as too simple – but if I pick out the most common successes my clients have used it for:

- 'Who would I be if . . . I could resist that cake?'
- 'Who would I be if . . . I was the kind of man who did go and speak to that girl?'
- 'Who would I be if . . . I was the kind of person who went for that job?'
- 'Who would I be if . . . I did get off my arse and go to the gym?'

- 'Who would I be if . . . I was the kind of person who wouldn't be treated that way?'

> **Task:**
>
> Next time you're faced with something where you would normally feel inhibited, or have something to do you consider impossible (but which other people can do), create a version of this question that fits the situation. Ask it of yourself. Notice what changes within you when you do – really focus on any and every change of thought, feeling and bodily expression. Especially the latter...

The physiology of excellence

When I ask myself 'Who would I be if I did/didn't . . . ?', and really pay attention to my response, I change physically – usually something subtle in my posture, sometimes in my stride, probably unnoticeable to anyone else, but I feel it. This physical change is something I coach my clients in when I teach them this. People often bandy about the mind/body connection in my line of work, with primacy nearly always being given to the mind, whereas actually it's much more of a two-way street.

Paul Ekman is a world authority on the relationship between emotions and our facial expressions. During one experiment he had volunteers pull a face that expressed for them one of seven different states – such as anger, sadness, fear and disgust. Because they were being photographed, the subject struck and held these poses for an extended period of time. And they started reporting that their mood was synching with their expression. Looking angry made them angrier. It seems our brain is looking for clues from the body about how it should be feeling and responding. In a way, our body is another bit of our environment to be interpreted.

NLP practitioners talk about the *physiology of excellence* – the body language that is most likely to produce your outcome in a particular situation. Top athletes are great at it; you can often tell who the winner is going to be just from the 'vibe' they give off – and who isn't going to win for the same reason. Your body is a powerful tool in your life-kit, so learn how to use it, listen to the shifts it brings in your thinking and your moods.

All of a sudden the old idea of 'fake it till you make it' gets some new paint. The writers of the classic song 'Smile (though your heart is aching)' were way ahead of their time – in fact a great way of reducing anxiety is to simply clamp a pen between your teeth. Researchers found that by doing so the mouth is forced to contort into a smile, and anxious subjects asked to do it reported their panic receding. **The brain follows where the body leads.**

The gentle adjustment of my physiology as I become 'the person I'd be if . . .' has an effect on my thoughts. With rehearsal, this physiology can become the new normality as it acts as the cement for a new behaviour, and even a new belief.

Parenting Tip: Fake it to make it

Teach your child early on that using their physiology to deliberately create a useful state is another thing that adds to their ILOC armoury. Teach them that how they feel is just an option, and they can choose another if it doesn't suit them. Kids tend to pick this idea up very quickly, like their different physiology is analogous to putting on the costume of their favourite superhero. Let them see you doing this yourself. Be a family of superheroes. When they're feeling confident or strong, get them to notice their posture, their breathing – everything about their physiology that is part of their state. The next time they feel nervous or lacking in confidence, remind them of those things, and get them to repeat them. The more they practise this 'physiology of excellence', the quicker they'll be able to access the positive state and banish the negative.

Just for today

A variation on the above, which is also very successful, is 'just for today':

- 'Just for today I'm going to pretend I'm good enough.'
- 'Just for today I'm going to assume that everything is happening for a good reason.'
- 'Just for today I'm going to think that everything will be fine.'
- 'Just for today I'm going to act like I'm having fun being me.'

Giving the change a short time frame makes it feel more manageable. It's what we call an 'as if' frame – an opportunity to just pretend that something is so, and, because we're not committing to it being true, we don't feel the same if we fail at it. I read somewhere that the film star Cary Grant was once asked how he became such a suave, confident man. His reply was, 'I just kept pretending until I didn't have to.' And he probably did it just one day at a time. So, just for today, what would you choose to be different?

Asking these questions isn't a magic wand to life's challenges. They are simply a tool that encourages you to be ILOC and to use your imagination to create a version of you that doesn't involve you being more of what you don't want to be.

You are who you think you are

Many years ago, a client with anorexia helped change the way I saw the world for ever. Chloe was seventeen years old, fantastically bright – as eating disorder girls usually are – and only 3lbs away from being sectioned under the Mental Health Act. She could barely manage stairs, had a face that looked as if a vacuum cleaner was plugged into the back of her head, and slunk in like a caricature of the classic teenager. She was a day patient at an NHS eating disorder clinic. She was at war with the staff who insisted that behavioural change – like adjusting her daily diet –

was the answer, while she was equally sure she needed to deal with the maelstrom that was her 'head stuff'. The first thing I had to agree to was that I wouldn't have anything to do with the clinic. They later accused me of being unprofessional by complying with her demand. She got better, so I live with their censure.

As I got to know Chloe I got to know her thoughts. She spoke of them, she texted them, and she wrote about them. I began to notice a difference between them. Some spoke of how she wanted to travel, to take photographs, to meet a boy. Others spoke of her ugliness, how unlovable she was, and how food was the enemy. Her body language seemed to reflect these different versions of her. The first walked in brightly with a dazzling smile, sat upright and engaged with me; the second dragged herself in, dropped into the chair, sulked and grunted.

I gave her a book to read by Professor Susan Blackmore called *The Meme Machine*. It develops an idea first put forward by Richard Dawkins that suggests that ideas compete for survival within our heads and our cultures in the same way that genes compete within nature – survival of the fittest. An easy example is comedy. Comedians very often come to prominence because they happen across a catchphrase that becomes contagious and spreads like wildfire around the country. The catchphrase is a meme, as are religions, as are political ideologies.

Professor Blackmore made the point that not all ideas or thoughts were beneficial to either the culture or the person holding them in their head. The idea of agriculture, for example, reduced the living standards of early farmers compared to hunter gatherers for a very long time. It's thought the trade-off for a harder life was the greater security that being able to live in larger numbers provided. At around the same time I began to see Chloe, I read about a virus that infects gypsy moth caterpillars and causes them to climb to the top of trees, where they die, liquefy, and drip virus-infected ooze down onto other caterpillars. A virus can hijack the behaviour of its host. The two ideas, memes and viruses, came together and became a subject of discussion between Chloe and me.

What would happen if someone got infected by a virus which caused them to change their thoughts about food so that they avoided it? What about if it wasn't an actual virus, but an idea, a meme, that spread from person to person? Anorexia has been around for a very long time. It's thought that Mary Queen of Scots suffered from it, but it was only after the death of singer Karen Carpenter in 1983 that the media brought it to widespread public attention – and the incidence of it rose accordingly. It sounded like a meme to me.

Chloe and I began to speak of her 'virus', the idea that was giving her the thoughts that maintained her illness. She began to write her thoughts down and highlighted the difference between virus thoughts and Chloe thoughts. She began to get stronger as she trained herself to respond to 'her' thoughts and ignore or argue against those of the virus. After eighteen months of working together Chloe backpacked around Australia, taking photographs and in the company of a boy, and with a healthy BMI. She's now a mother of three and a Cognitive Hypnotherapist who specialises in, guess what? Eating disorders. I've successfully used variations of the meme idea with a good number of other people with eating disorders and other problems that are thought-generated suggestions i.e. most of the people I see.

If you're aware of having a 'virus' try these:

Work the Problem

- Write down the thoughts you're having about something where you think the virus is at work.
- Get a highlighter and mark the thoughts that are 'virus' thoughts.
- Get another highlighter and mark down those which feel more like your own.
- Beside each 'virus' thought write down everything you can think of as to why it isn't true.
- Beside each of your own thoughts, write down everything you can think of to support it.

Over time I've found people get better at identifying virus thoughts as they happen and improve their ability to disregard them. After all, any thought you have isn't your own until you've acted on it, it's just your brain throwing thoughts at you.

Our brains have only a finite ability to focus on anything in particular, and we know by now that they're creatures of habit. If your brain's grown used to being in protection mode, then the Prover will mostly bring to your attention things interpreted to be threatening. The world you live in will feel negative because you feed that negativity with your attention preference. The same goes for your self-esteem, you feed your confidence by focusing on the things that build it, and starve it by focusing on your failures. And the more of these things you notice, of either stripe, the more you will.

Over time, whichever version of ourselves we focus on the most becomes the strongest, and what becomes weak becomes irrelevant. Once you recognise that your brain is a thought factory, churning out responses to what it thinks is happening to you, then you can begin to do two things: choose which thoughts belong to you (and by doing so ignore those that don't), and focus your attention on them in order to encourage your brain to have more of them. If we are the sum total of the thoughts we have about ourselves, then why not begin to make sure we have the thoughts that create the version of ourselves we have the most fun being?

The story so far

In this section, I've focused on you:

- How to tune your brain to the frequency of growth through ILOC.
- How to free yourself from the tyranny of beliefs that keep

you in unnecessary protection.
- How you can make a choice to be who you want to be.
- How you can be the creator of your own character.

Not only will this change your life for the better, but it will create an environment for those within your influence to do the same. You will be an exemplar for your children and, as the years go on, the family feedback loop could create something extraordinary.

Imagine a world where children learn from an early age that they're in charge of their feelings, that they have tools to change an emotion they don't want to have.

Imagine if you taught them from the viewpoint of being able to guide the kind of reality they create, one painted by their brains in the colours of growth.

Imagine if you learned to interpret their behaviour as just a response to the reality their brain was creating in that moment. Imagine how much flexibility that would give you in helping them search for ways to change it and so change their experience.

Let's now go on to directly looking at what we can do to nurture resilience and growth in your children.

PART III:
GROWING YOUR CHILD

In Part I I developed a model of how the mind works to create both our world and our sense of identity within it. I made the argument for the things we don't like ourselves for – our limitations and shortcomings – being the result of glitches in the software of our brain that predominantly arise during childhood.

I went on to describe how these glitches are being used by our consumer society to get us to behave in ways that serve that society, but which often cause us to feel stressed, depressed, anxious, unfulfilled, or just plain unhappy. If you begin to view things in the way I suggest, you'll realise that a great many things you've assumed to be true are made up, especially the ideas you have about yourself. Not only are they made up, but they continue to be made up on a moment-by-moment basis. It leads to an unconscious assumption that things are just the way they are, including you, and that change is difficult.

However, implicit within my model is the notion that if things aren't true, then they can be changed. We can correct the glitches, we can take control of our own narrative, we can create ourselves as the illusion we'd have most fun being. We might not be able to make our life what we want it to be, but we can make it what we want it to be about.

I only wish I had known what I'm writing about now when I became a father. The opportunity you have as a parent knowing this stuff can be life-changing for your child. Your children give you the chance, every day, to help them grow. You can guide them in how they see the world, in how they view themselves, in how they treat others, and in the lessons you want them to learn. Knowing how their young minds work isn't to be used to keep them from challenges, or situations where they could experience a Significant Emotional Event. Good parenting is about being brave, not cosseting your child from life's buffeting. It's about helping them get themselves back up when life has knocked them down, developing the mindset that will serve them throughout their lives in keeping them resilient, flexible, and happy in themselves. It's not going to be easy, but it is possible.

Part II was all about your own personal development, about the things you could do to make yourself exemplify the traits you'd like your children to grow up with. I think you'll soon see how they begin to fit into the way you interact with your family; as you change, so will they. Now it's time to turn our attention on growing your children. I've broken the next part of the book into eight sections into which I've poured everything I could think of to help you with the toughest job in the world. Thank goodness it pays so well. As in Part II, I've included little exercises to help you turn the ideas contained in each mantra into habits of thinking that will guide your actions automatically – if you put the effort into using them. But I have high hopes, you've impressed me a lot so far.

8 Mantras for parents

Dear Parents

These are the things I want to share with you based on what I've learned from being a therapist and a parent. There are eight mantras I hope you'll soon start chanting to keep your sanity and poise throughout parenthood:

MANTRA 1: You're training them or they're training you.

MANTRA 2: They're not who they're going to be yet.

MANTRA 3: Rewards don't always reward them.

MANTRA 4: It's good to give them less.

MANTRA 5: Life is what you make it mean.

MANTRA 6: They're not difficult, they're just not you.

MANTRA 7: ILOC takes bravery.

MANTRA 8: Don't expect.

MANTRA 1:

You're training them or they're training you

Tattoo this mantra on your eyelids so it gets embedded in your brain while you sleep. Now, I risk getting lynched by a vengeful parent group, but once you understand the young causal brain of your children it should really simplify how you raise them in the early years. The causal mechanism of the brain evolved to predict stuff, like 'What happens if I do that?' **From very early on your children are trying to figure out how the world works – especially how the world works _for them_.** As soon as they can move they start exploring their physical boundaries, what they can reach and where they can crawl, as well as their social boundaries – what they can do and what they can't do, what brings approval from others, and what leads to its withdrawal.

I marvel in the supermarket at parents who surrender to the screaming of their child by rewarding them with the thing they were demanding. Who is training who? The child – imagine them as a young not-so-mad scientist – is trying an experiment based around 'How can I get what I want?' He or she is likely to try out a range of behaviours, all based upon 'What gets me the result?' Does looking cute do it? Does asking for it do it? Does saying please at the end of the request do it? Does screaming the place down do it? Children generally have a greater degree of behavioural flexibility than adults – we care too much about what other people think – so joining them on the floor in the frozen section and kicking and screaming louder doesn't seem much of an option. Children often win just by attrition, and by the parent justifying that it's just this once. It never is! Kids are great at one-time learning. Unless part of that learning is that there isn't always a 'yes' from a parent at the end of their experiments, and that not getting everything they want is a part of the way the world works, then you're in for hell. **You're training them, or they're training you.** Chant it, meditate it, turn it into a T-shirt, because if you want any quality of life as a parent, and to actually produce kids who are fun to have around, the training needs to swing heavily in your favour. The clients I've seen who had a childhood without a 'no' boundary, present with a range of issues. To begin with, they're universally ELOC. The world is expected to provide, they just have to behave in a way that encourages the world to pony up. Some will demand it aggressively – bully, shout and scream to get their own way – some will depend on pity, illness or helplessness to get their needs met. Not a single case is pretty to watch in action and, if the parents are still alive, my clients tend to still be shouting at them, or wheedling something out of them, for as long as either one of them is drawing breath. I think *no* is one of the most important words in a parent's vocabulary, to be used rarely when it's about the child's potential or the pursuit of their dreams, but often when it's about the acquisition of 'stuff', or a demand for you to do something they could do for themselves. It's vital that children learn that sometimes it's their turn to get nothing, that it's someone else's turn to get something, that life isn't fair or equal, that there is winning and losing, and no means no. The one place a child doesn't belong in the family is in charge.

There is a process called *adaptation* by which children adapt their beliefs and behaviour in response to the messages they're given, or the way they interpret the message. When I was a child I got strong messages about respecting authority. Children were to be seen and not heard, all adults were called uncle or auntie – never by their first name alone – and children stood so adults could sit. My adapting to that left me quite over-awed when I joined the police, quite intimidated to be working with people who I saw as the pinnacle of authority. Imagine my surprise and confusion when I had things thrown at me by children who had adapted to a very different message about the police. You need to be aware of how young this flow of adaptation can begin.

New parents are, understandably, a bit overwhelmed by the pressure of getting things right, so from the start they can begin to respond by doing more of whatever seems to be working. Not a bad way to calibrate what you're doing, really, but mistakes can easily be made. If, for example, the baby seems to settle better in bed with you, or sleep better on you than in their cot, it's tempting to continue to do so. But if you begin to adapt everything you do because that's what the baby prefers, he or she never learns to adapt to things that aren't ideal. The principle is established that if there is any bending to do, it's the parents who do it. That will not go well long-term. If you want them to learn to sleep in the cot it might cost you some sleepless nights, but the baby will adapt.

I also want to mention consistency. It is vital that your word is impeccable. Say what you mean, mean what you say. Don't deviate beyond the chances you say you're going to give them and be consistent in the boundaries you set. Children are actually much happier once they know where the border of acceptable conduct is. If it varies according to your mood they get confused, they can get anxious, and most of all they spot the opportunity to grab some real estate – 'but you let us stay up late last night', etc. If clear and solid boundaries are set then peace can reign, if they appear to be porous then your kids will turn into Genghis Khan as they exploit what they see as your weakness. Also, be consistent with your partner. Divide and rule is the aim of your children so you must unite. Agree on the approach, compromise with each other where you should, but be immovable together.

Bear in mind that explaining to a child under five years old why what they did was wrong is pretty much a waste of time if you're looking to influence their behaviour through it. Their brains haven't come on-line enough to understand reasoning beyond the black and white of some-thing being good or bad, right or wrong, loved or unloved.

When I hear a mother saying to little Juliet, 'You really shouldn't have pinched your brother like that because it wasn't a nice thing to do, you wouldn't like it done to you, would you?', it makes me smile. Juliet is just waiting for the words to end. The words are the punishment, and they're not so bad.

However, I think it's a great idea to talk to your child about these things from an early age, to set out moral and ethical causal relationships such as 'It's not nice to do that because . . .', or 'I want you to behave like this because . . .' Research has shown that the more words they hear the better they're going to do in school (by the age of three, a child living in poverty will have heard thirty million fewer words than a child from a professional family). Children are sponges for cause and effect and equivalence. So let them soak up the lessons on how to behave from the earliest of opportunities. But don't mistake these explanations, or tellings off, for punishment that will necessarily change their behaviour, because it's likely to go over their undeveloped heads. Explain, definitely, and *then* sanction.

I think the animal kingdom can sometimes be a good place to look for wisdom we consider ourselves too clever to need to copy. If you look at dogs, mums chastise their pups in two ways, a quick cuff round the ear or isolation. The first is no longer acceptable in our culture, but the second is a powerful tool if used appropriately. If you look at horses, mares whose foals are trying their patience send them out of the herd. For a social animal, it's viscerally dangerous to have the security of company withdrawn –

there are wolves out there in the ancestral memory – so the naughty step, or time in a room alone without toys or video games, is very powerful. They don't need long, leaving them to stew in the desert of your disapproval for too long can be something they might turn into a Significant Emotional Event. It's just to mark a cause and effect boundary you want them to respect. I suggest five minutes for young ones, ten to fifteen minutes once they're verbal. Get the training right in the early years and they'll be self-directing later. Get it wrong, and you'll be running yourself ragged for years.

Meditating on Mantra 1:

It's easy for appreciation to drift into expectation. Reflect on the balance of giving and receiving

- What positive beliefs and behaviours have you instilled in your children?
- What negative beliefs and behaviours have you trained them into without meaning to?
- How could you adapt your training to change that?
- Looking at your family in this way, what expectations of your children are you meeting that they've trained you into?
- Are those expectations healthy? If not, how could you change them?

MANTRA 2:

They're not who they're going to be yet

When I look at the modern mothers' movement it seems to be incredibly pressured – almost as if the clock has turned back to the 1950s and mothers are measuring themselves against some impossible standard of domestic mistressy (yes, I just made that word up, 'mastery' seemed sexist). I see so many knackered mothers on Facebook who are catching forty winks beside the pool while their child has a swimming lesson on the way to an astrophysics tutor. Everyone is working so hard to live up to some ideal of a perfect parent, and of course the child is the symbol of their success in that role. That's as much pressure on the child as it is on the parents, so no wonder they don't have time for an actual childhood. My message to parents is: chill.

Whatever you do, no matter how hard you work to be perfect, your child will confound you by being imperfect in return. They are going to grow up with some issues and some learned limitations. Some of those they'll get from their interactions with you. To your kids you're a bit of a god early on, so your every word carries a lot of weight.

Sometimes your words are going to be dumb, and sometimes your children will misunderstand your meaning.

I get parents ringing reasonably often asking if I can help their child with a problem, like being scared of the dark, or eating more vegetables.

If it's a fear that is really disturbing the child then obviously I'll help, but what I'm cognisant of is the role such challenges play in us learning to be ILOC. If a child learns that every time a problem pops up in life Uncle Trevor will wave a wand and make it go away, he or she will grow into an adult who still waits for someone to take care of life's challenges for them. Read this, and then again, and tattoo it on your eyelids underneath the 'you're training them or they're training you' one: **They're not who they're going to be yet.** It's so important I'm going to type it twice. **They're not who they're going to be yet.** My children are over thirty and there are still days I chant it. We are always in a state of becoming. This is never more true than when we're children. How can you know that the thing about them that you're worrying about, like going through a phase of being scared of the dark, isn't going to be the very thing that teaches them something that defines their adult character? Give your child some space to solve or grow out of the problems they're struggling with on their own. If they fall, let them find their own way back to their feet. By all means let them know you're there, but instantly rescuing them can lead to them still expecting you to do so when they're thirty.

Recently I had the privilege of watching a tribe of

monkeys from the comfort of a poolside sun lounger in Sri Lanka. At one point I heard a baby monkey, who'd wandered away from the group for a drink out of the pool, crying plaintively for its mother. After a few calls the mother responded, not by running up to the baby, but by moving to a place in its eye-line about twenty feet away. It seemed a deliberate move with an obvious message: I'm here, but help yourself. The baby scampered over and was rewarded with a hug for taking action.

I remember having the 'help' of a young niece in the garden many years ago. She must have been about eight. She was digging with a little spade, and her sunglasses kept slipping off her nose. Eventually that annoyed her enough to do something about it and she took them off. Then she looked at me and handed them in my direction. 'I don't want them,' I said. She thought for a moment, looked around, and then put them back on her nose! ELOC. Had I been better at parenting then I'd have said, 'What can you do with them instead?' and guided her towards her own solution. As validation of my message that they're not who they're going to be, we recently had lunch with her. She's now a wonderful, vibrant woman in her early twenties who is doing bar work to support herself while at university. We'd heard that she'd recently dislocated her shoulder when she fell carrying buckets of bottles of wine from the cellar. What we hadn't heard is how she responded. 'I didn't want to make a fuss, so I banged it back in against a wall.' She's come a long way from the little girl with the sunglasses. We're not who we're going to be yet.

It's my strong contention that solving your children's problems for them deprives them of a vital life-skill, just as trying to keep them from the heartbreak of failure will leave them unprepared for adulthood. That's why I'm so opposed to the school fad of not allowing competitive sports and having sports days where 'everyone wins'. If you keep children away from failure and give them an illusion that the world is like that, then life after school can come as a huge shock. Raising our children to believe that they're the centre of the universe – even the centre of the family – is similarly counter-productive. So many children seem to feel that the world owes them a living and I place the blame on the cult of 'the wonder that is my child'. Narcissism – destructive self-love – has increased significantly in recent generations, and the author of a book called *Generation Me*, Jean Twenge, has this to say about it, '... *the most common pattern was overindulgent parenting (overpraising, putting the child on a pedestal, permissiveness and little discipline) leading to narcissism later in life*'. Being told by your parents that you're unreservedly wonderful and that your every scribble is Shakespeare is Just. Plain. Wrong. No wonder the poor dears leave school expecting the world to fall at their feet in gratitude for turning up, and get a slap in the face with a huge wet fish when that same world actually asks them to prove their value. Refer to what I said earlier about embracing failure and teach them that mindset instead.

As a child, the rule in my parents' house was that 'children should be seen and not heard'. I don't agree with that.

In mine they had a voice, but not an equal one. Our household didn't revolve around their needs. Sometimes they missed out on things because it didn't suit us or someone else had to come first, while at other times we bent ourselves out of shape to put them first. It was a series of compromises, and the reasons for those compromises were made clear to them. They didn't always agree with them, or see our point of view, but at least they were learning that there were reasons involving other people that needed to be considered. That's not what I see in so many families today. I think it's time to redress the balance somewhat and restore the primacy of the adults in the household.

Meditating on Mantra 2:

- What do I worry about in regard to my child?
- Are those worries likely to still be a problem when they're adults?
- How could you turn them into learning opportunities for them now?
- What strengths of theirs could be developed here, and how?

MANTRA 3:

Rewards don't always reward them

Until recently, science only recognised two drives that motivate us, biological and environmental – basically food, sex and shelter to cover our survival needs; and things like money, goods, praise, the loss of something and avoidance of criticism or withdrawal of approval to cover our environmental ones. As you can see, they're all things dependent on, or to do with, the outside world, and for that reason are known as *extrinsic* motivators. They also comprise most of the carrot and stick ways people try to motivate others. From the carrot of a bonus, or money for passing exams, to the stick of the threat of the sack or the withdrawal of the Playstation, it's the classic way of getting people – including your children – to do stuff. And it doesn't work that well, which is odd. The pleasure principle suggests that we do more of what rewards us, yet overwhelming research proves that externally incentivised people are less productive than those who do things for their own reasons, or for free. 'If-then' rewards or punishments (i.e. *if* you pass your maths test *then* we'll give you £10) may increase your child's performance in the short term, but the child will tend to lose interest in the task or subject in the long term. So giving them a treat for sticking with their piano lessons might get them through their music grades, but might put them off continuing to play the instrument for life. Also, the dopamine released for a reward tends to diminish over time, so the reward has to keep escalating to get the same effect.

So how do you get your kids to clean their rooms? To begin with, make it non-negotiable. It is going to be done, and by them. When they've got over that trauma there are three things that tend to squeeze the best out of people carrying out any routine or mundane task. First of all, give them a reason for needing to do it. Our causative brain means we're suckers for reasons. The word 'because' is nearly magical in its effect (unless it's followed by . . . 'I said so'). In a classic experiment a queue of people were waiting to use a busy photocopier in an office. A woman came in with a sheet of paper and asked 'Is it ok if I go first?' As you might expect, even in Britain, the answer was a singular no. Experimenters waited until the queue was refreshed with new people and then repeated the request, with one change. This time the woman added, 'because I've only got one copy'. Amazingly 60% of the new queue agreed – even though some of them only had one copy too! *Because* has a lot of power. If you want your kids to clean their rooms give them a reason. If it can also be a reason that would be important to them, so much the better, and 'because it's a health hazard' doesn't count.

Secondly, acknowledge that the job is boring. Empathy can go a long way. Thirdly, allow them to do it their way.

Not only does this fit with the goal of building resilience, but it's also been shown that not being instructed on how to do it increases our willingness to do things. Give them the task, then leave them to work out the details of how they're going to achieve it.

As an aside, here's a little bit of knowledge that might help. It begins with a little story. My son Stuart used to drive me mad. I'd go into his bedroom, look at the evidence that the apocalypse had begun and say to him 'Wow, this bedroom is a mess'. He'd look up from his computer, do me the courtesy of looking around the room as if it was as big a surprise to him, and agree. Mollified, I'd walk away. An hour later I'd walk in and hit the roof. 'I thought I told you to clean this room up!' Stu would protest in hard-to-believe surprise, 'No you didn't!' 'Yes I did. Now clean it up.' 'Ok,' he'd agree in a teenage way that suggested that this is the worst thing that could happen to anyone, ever. But he wouldn't move. 'Go on then,' I'd prod. 'I am,' he'd say. 'I mean now. This moment. Immediately.' Finally there'd be movement. His body, my blood pressure.

It was only when I heard about a certain difference between people that I understood what was happening. People, as a generalisation, tend to be one of two things, either *literal*, or *inferential*. If I said to you 'I'm thirsty' and you replied 'Oh, are you?' it might be an indicator that you're a literal person – you're just taking my words at face value, as information. If, however, you replied 'Oh, are you, would you like a drink?' then you may be more inferential – looking within people's words for a call to action. This is important to know in any relationship. To an inferential person, saying to their partner 'I really like those' while pointing at something in a shop window a week before your birthday is the same as putting a big neon-lit finger over the item with a sign saying, 'This is what I want!' But if you're with a literal you're probably going to open your eyes on the big day to a random jumper. Conversely, literals call a spade a spade and say exactly what they want. Back when I was in the police, I remember a female officer on my shift, who was transferring to another station, came in to the briefing one morning clutching an Argos catalogue. She announced to those assembled, 'Look, you all know I'm going, and that there'll be a collection, so this is what I want', and pointed us towards an item of jewellery handily ringed with biro. And out she swept. I now realise it was the inferential people who didn't put in for her collection. I was one of them. Rude.

Inferentials find literal people abrasive, rude in their directness, and completely lacking in social subtlety. They find it hard to say directly what they want and tend to hint, or ask in a roundabout way. Inferential, even. Literals find inferentials obtuse, vague and wishy-washy. They feel like they're expected to be mind-readers. 'Don't ask don't get' is their motto. Going back to my son's room you can see what was happening. I'm inferential. To me, saying 'Wow, this bedroom is a mess' is a clear and unambiguous instruction. To my literal son it's just a factual comment. In fact, he's so literal that 'now' doesn't necessarily mean this moment. Things improved greatly once we realised this about the both of us. He learned to avoid direct requests because they tended to trigger a refusal, and I learned to tell him very clearly what my expectation of him was. I'm imagining a lot of light bulbs going on at this moment.

Returning to motivation, something that can transform a child's motivation is what's called the Sawyer Effect, in honour of Tom, who got his friends to paint a fence he'd been tasked to do by persuading them that it was fun. In the words of Mark Twain, '*Work consists of whatever a body is obliged to do, and play consists of whatever a body is not obliged to do.*' If you can make a task fun, or seemingly play, then much of the effort of doing it disappears. It's why many promising young amateur athletes 'burn out' once the fun of competition is replaced by the unrelenting focus that is required in professional sport. When a sports person stops enjoying what they're doing they're likely to lose the edge that made them great at it.

It's a bit of a shock to find that the traditional tools for getting your children to do something you think is useful or necessary aren't actually very effective. Yet when you look at how long we haven't been very good at getting our kids to do what we ask, it shouldn't be a surprise; it's as if it's passed down to us as good parenting practice without anyone actually checking its efficacy. But there is something that works better. It's called *intrinsic* motivation, let me explain.

One thing you can pretty much take for granted with a child is their curiosity. A professor called Richard Ryan claims 'If there's anything fundamental about our nature, it's the capacity for interest. Some things facilitate it. Some things undermine it.' I think that's true for the vast majority of people, and I've felt sorry for the few people I've met who seem to show no curiosity about anything. Self-Determination Theory is an approach to motivation which echoes many of the properties of ILOC. It was first developed by Edward Deci and the aforementioned Richard Ryan, Professor at Rochester University. Deci highlights six key components of intrinsic motivation when he says, '**We have an inherent tendency to seek out *novelty* and *challenges*, to *extend and increase our capabilities*, to *explore* and to *learn*.**'

That's:

- Novelty
- Challenges
- Extend capabilities
- Increase capabilities
- Explore
- Learn

Do you notice that every single one of those is a 'Grow' word?

It's with these six elements that we can engage our children in learning, and teach them how to motivate themselves throughout their lives. In any situation you want to motivate them ask yourself:

'What is there that's new for them to experience and explore that would challenge them in some way and grow their abilities?'

Each situation will offer differing opportunities to focus on one, more or all of these magnificent six. There is possibility in every situation – at least, if you believe there is you're more likely to find it. Many big discoveries have come from an individual doing something that many have done before them but spotting something new within it. I can guarantee one of those six Grow ingredients would have been present in their mindset. Your challenge as a parent is to guide your child using these ingredients whenever they face a challenge, but **without being too directive** – and I'll tell you why that's important. **A sense of autonomy is vital for intrinsic motivation, a sense of acting from a feeling of choice and personal volition.** Research has shown it leads to better grades at school, enhanced persistence at any activity, better productivity, fewer occasions of burnout, and a greater sense of wellbeing. So feeling in control of your choices is a big deal. It synchronises with my message of ILOC perfectly. Wherever possible (and of course that will depend on the task and the age of the child) give them as much control over a task as possible, including the timeframe, the method used to accomplish it, and the people they do it with. The more choice they feel in each of these areas the more likely they are to be self-motivated in completing it. When I apply this to my son and his room, what I should have done was give him a timeframe by which I wanted the task completed, let him know what materials were available, seen if there was a way of making it fun or competitive, and found a benefit to him doing it that didn't involve extrinsic reward.

When you consider that the Alacaluf people of Patagonia encourage children as young as four to fend for themselves, hunting shellfish with a spear and cooking their own dinner, you can see we make very different assumptions about our children's ability to make their own choices. And the Alacaluf kids aren't struggling with depression and anxiety. So, at every stage of their childhood ask yourself, 'How much can we hand over to them to be responsible for?' As it becomes a habit, you might be amazed how independent they become and how much they thrive because of it.

Meditating on Mantra 3:

In situations that suit this theme ask yourselves:

- What is there here that's new for them to experience and explore that would challenge them in some way and grow their abilities?
- How much can we hand over to them to be responsible for?
- Which of the six Grow ingredients will be most useful here?
- In situations like holidays (at home or away) what new experience can be created that would be a stretch for them in terms of the above?
- Each month, pick one of the six Grow ingredients and discuss together what family project could be pursued, either together or individually. At the end of the month have some family time reporting on progress. If this is done regularly, picking a goal and measuring progress towards it will become a productive habit.
- Look at the assumptions that lie behind what is 'safe' for them to do or not do. Are they actually true? Could you trust your children with more responsibility?

MANTRA 4:

It's good to give them less

I wonder when it became the parent's responsibility to make sure their child wasn't bored? When their every moment had to be filled with some entertainment or you were somehow failing as a parent? So many children are surrounded by so many things to engage them that they never learn how to entertain themselves. I think that's a shame because it's where the seeds of a creative adult come from. When you give a baby a wrapped present what does it usually end up doing? That's right, it plays with the box as much as the present. At that stage the difference between them hasn't been learned. They're equal in possibility, and that possibility is limited only by the child's imagination.

Without even realising it, by giving them more, we begin to limit our children's imaginations as the less they have to imagine. My favourite toy as a child was Action Man. Many birthdays were given over to gaining more uniforms for him, but they never covered all my interests. I remember turning him into a knight by making a shield and helmet out of the centre of a toilet roll, his armour from a frog-man's wetsuit that I drew chainmail onto, and I found a handy cocktail stick that looked like a little sword. Looking back now I realise that my absorption in that activity contained many of the ingredients for building intrinsic motivation, as well as introducing something that enhances creativity: constraints. If my parents had bought me a knight's outfit my opportunity to create would have been clearly reduced to zero. If I had had access to *any* material I needed to make it, that too, a little counter-intuitively, would have reduced my creativity. Research has shown that introducing constraints – some kind of limit – to an activity increases our imagination. Having a few items to make a knight's costume forced my brain to come up with novel solutions that challenged me and caused me to explore a number of different possibilities. As a result my capabilities expanded.

I had the privilege of visiting my favourite artist in her studio on the north Norfolk coast. Rachel Lockwood is a brilliant naturalist painter and I discovered that she had three or four different paintings on the go at any one time, from initial sketching through to sitting with it a while to see if it was finished. One thing she shared about her artistic process really stood out for me. She said, 'I get excited when I draw a line and just see where it takes me.' The line isn't of anything, not the edge of a leaf or the belly of a hare, it's just a line. She then lets her imagination turn it into something. The rest of the painting emerges from that initial constraint. Drawing a squiggle on a page and telling your child to turn it into an animal would be an equivalent thing.

Learning about the value of constraints led to a new

appreciation of my dad. All his life he's been a master bodger. I've never seen him do a job properly using the right tools or materials, but what he does works, even if it isn't always pretty. I've often thought that if he could do it 'properly' he wouldn't, he just seems to enjoy the bodge too much. I now realise what a valuable skill he taught me – and what a creative man he is. **Teaching your child to make do with what's available is a cornerstone of producing a creative adult.**

So give them less. Give them things that aren't the product of someone else's imagination. Give them things that they can make something else out of. Lego sets are great. There's a place for learning to follow the instructions to make a space station out of it in the image of the person who designed the set, but there's also great value in sitting down with an assortment of bits and guiding your child to make *their* idea of a space station.

Give them time. Creative people spend a lot of time staring into space. As Jackie Chan remarked in his role as Mr Han in the remake of the *Karate Kid*, 'Being still and doing nothing are two very different things.' I've used that on my wife a lot. We have two styles of thinking. The first is quick, verbal and 'left-brained'. We tend to value it a lot in our culture. The second is slower, often works through imagery and metaphor, and is more right-brained. While we encourage our children to focus and concentrate, and in class take that to be the signs of a good student, it's the one who appears distracted, who doodles and who doesn't seem to be sticking to the task who is the more likely to come up with something new. A child who stares into space might be the child who invents the warp drive that will take us there. History is littered with moments of reverie that have led to huge discoveries.

The road marker 46.58 on Highway 128 in the States identifies a pretty nondescript piece of road, but it's where an outstanding moment of insight was recorded. Kary Mullis is a biochemist who was wrestling with a major challenge of molecular biology. On a long night time drive, with the windscreen washers on, he left his mind to mull over ideas he was having until, in a moment of clarity, a discovery came to him. 46.58 is where he pulled over to scribble it down. It is called PCR (for polymerase chain reaction). You've probably never heard of it, but the genome would have taken years longer to sequence without it. It's used extensively for medical and forensic diagnosis. It's so important that the *New York Times* described it as, '. . . highly original and significant, virtually dividing biology into the two epochs of before PCR and after PCR'. Not impressed yet? His company awarded him a $10,000 bonus. Still not? They earned $300 million when they sold the patent. It was his turn not to be impressed. Even winning the Nobel prize doesn't take the sting out of that.

Sometimes ideas have to bubble and ferment awhile before coming to the conscious surface. Leaving kids time to stare, rather than have to follow a revision wall planner, helps to develop that slower habit of thinking that produces so much, and frees you from the tyranny of feeling that you have to fill their day. Imagine that, your life free of the feeling that you're failing them if they're bored, or somehow a bad parent if they're not always busy with clubs and activities. Let them learn that boredom is their choice. Let them discover what comes from silence and self-reliance.

Give them less so they learn to create more.

Meditating on Mantra 4:

Ask yourself questions like:

- How often do I make things easy for my children?
- How could I introduce more 'productive struggle' into their activities?
- What is my response to their boredom? Does it serve them?
- How could I introduce a constraint that would make them have to solve a problem or be creative?

MANTRA 5:

Life is what you make it mean

Socrates once said that the unexamined life wasn't worth living. I don't know about that, but I do think an examined life can make it better. I've described how the brain creates our impression of reality from the way it connects things from the present moment to things from our past, and creates an anticipation of what the future will hold as a consequence. I've also suggested that who we think ourselves to be is largely the result of our life story needing a character; that actually our sense of self is just a figment of the mind that is, in a way, simply the sum of the person who has had your life experiences. It follows, then, that if you could change your memories you could change your sense of self, and that's exactly what Cognitive Hypnotherapy proposes is possible.

We know our plastic brain is learning and changing from before you were born to the moment of your death. It has shown that our memories are not written in stone, or stored away in a filing cabinet, or even accurate. It's been suggested that just recalling a memory changes it because it's being seen through your current perceptions. I've worked with scores of clients with traumatic or disturbing memories who have, in a short space of time, been able to view them more dispassionately, and where the effect of those past events have ceased to be felt in their lives. I completely believe in our ability to change the perception of our past, and to thus change our perception of ourselves in the present. Wouldn't it be great if children learned how to interpret what is happening to them as it happens so that things don't have the chance to become butterfly events and grow up into something bigger? While it's impossible to stop that happening in its entirety (and any therapist reading this just let out their breath), we can provide our children with tools which enable them to develop a sense of ILOC through reflecting on things that happen to them and guiding their brain to create the right causal conclusions or the most appropriate equivalences. I talked about encouraging a positive explanatory style earlier with the question, 'How is this not about me?' This is about developing that skill.

Getting the narrative right

Let's start with teaching children to be the editors of their story. Kids make everything about themselves, so the object of reframing a negative event in a positive way is twofold: to not make it about 'themselves', and to prime them with what positives could come from it.

If your child comes home unhappy because of an upset with a person, a friend or a teacher for example, these are good reframing questions (by reframing I mean helping someone see the situation from a different perspective), that I've found can help:

1. How was what happened not about you as a person? (How was it about others, or the situation, or their *behaviour* rather than about their self.)
2. Would you behave that way towards someone else?
3. What is it about them that makes them behave that way?
4. So was it about you as a person, or something to do with them?
5. Are you happy with your response? What would you do differently next time?
6. Is there anything that would stop you from doing that?
7. Does it have to stop you, really? (You can introduce the question 'Who would you be if . . . it didn't stop you?' which can be very powerful.)

Obviously how these questions play out will depend on the responses you get and the situation you're dealing with. I don't intend these questions to be followed like a recipe, more as things to guide your intention in making this not about their ok-ness.

If they are upset about an event – like not passing something or not getting picked for a team, try:

1. What made you deserve this?
2. What didn't make you deserve this?
3. What can you learn from this that will get you what you want later?

4. What's the first thing you can do to get started with this?
5. What qualities do you have that will help you?
6. What would you like more of?
7. What can you do to get more of what you just answered?

These questions are steered for children in their teens, when they're capable of this kind of analysis. If they're pre-teen, listen for the connections they make about what happens and reframe those – i.e. listen for their 'becauses' and their equivalences.

The reflective process

The idea of getting kids to focus on their qualities is a good one. If I ask my clients what they like about themselves they'll often manage a fair imitation of a goldfish, before finally spluttering out something about being kind to animals. If I change tack and ask them what they *don't* like about themselves they'll have no problem writing an extensive list. Encouraging your children to become more aware of their strengths and qualities helps to strengthen them, and learn to use them, and trust them. A student of mine, Tom, told me of an interesting exercise he and his wife Jill did, which I would encourage you to do with your own children if you feel they are of an appropriate age and temperament. When their daughter Holly was eleven, and just starting secondary school, they thought it would be a good confidence boost for her to have a list of things that they and her younger sister thought she was good at. The list included:

Piano	*Violin*
Being kind	*Singing*
Games / sport	*Caring for people*
Dance	*Understanding other people's feelings*
Being gorgeous	*Being a good citizen*
Looking after others	*Being beautiful*
Being talented	*Being reliable*
Being determined	*Being courageous*
Swimming	*Being fair*
Sharing	*Being a good friend*
Running	*Being a good sister*
BEING HOLLY!	

They then printed it off and placed it on her wardrobe door where she would see it every day, just as a reminder if ever she felt low or in need of reassurance.

Then, when Holly was thirteen, Tom found that several items on the list had been crossed out. Specifically,

Piano
Being gorgeous
Being beautiful
Being a good friend

In his words, 'I was initially quite shocked, especially with respect to those concerning her self-image. "Piano" I understood, as she had stopped playing. We knew she had been through one of those tough times within her friendship group so that the "good friend" made sense too. What this allowed us to do was to sit down with her and have a "What's that all about?" conversation. We were quite surprised how low her self-esteem had become and how this seemed to correlate and depend so much (in her world) on the school/friendship situation. There was strong evidence that what she perceived her friends thought about her was more potent than what Mum and Dad said.'

Tom and his wife were able to renegotiate the list, only allowing those things that Holly was happy to include.

On reflection they felt the benefits had been:

- It provided a regular reminder of her abilities. We live in a society which does not encourage celebrating our skills, which, in fact, considers such acts as boastful.
- Helped her to develop her identity.
- Something for her just to look at when feeling low and full of self-doubt.
- It provided them with a warning that something was wrong.
- The renegotiation process provided a great opportunity to communicate about the things that were concerning her that Tom and his wife might otherwise be unaware of.

This exercise by Tom and Jill reminded me of something I'd seen only the week before on a trip to Amsterdam. We went to the Anne Frank museum – definitely a must-see with your children once they're her age. It was an immensely moving experience. At the end is a short film where her father, Otto, talks about reading her diary for the first time and his surprise at what he found within it. He'd felt he was very close to Anne, yet much of what he read was unknown to him. He concluded by saying he doubted whether anybody really knows their children. If you think about how much your parents don't know about you, it's hard to disagree with him. Being a part of your child's reflective process might go some way to rectifying that. So, in addition to Tom's exercise, I suggest the following – and I mean this mainly for children of secondary school age: get all of the family to write down the positive attributes of everyone else. Have a list for every member.

When any of you achieve anything positive that is noticeable to the rest of the family, look at that person's attribute list and see what there is on the list that was a factor in the achievement. Anybody is free to call attention to an achievement, not just the person who has done it (this is to prevent introverts from hiding their light). Feel free to add more to the lists as you go. Look for reasons to include persistence and determination – I'll explain why towards the end of the book. Make this a family ritual, a feedback session on the achievements of all of you, so the emphasis isn't just on your children and they learn to see childhood as part of a greater process. If you refer back to my earlier point that you feed what you focus on, you'll see why this exercise can be so important.

Nearly always look on the bright side of life

A pessimist sees the difficulty in every opportunity; an optimist sees the opportunity in every difficulty.

Winston Churchill

A few final points about reflection and how it links to our belief systems. It's important to listen to the beliefs your children verbalise to explain the reason things happen and how they feel about them – what I've previously described as their explanatory style. Always be aware of how easy it is in their early years to pass yours on to them; after all, that's a major part of parenting. It's no coincidence that most people who believe their religion is the true one just happen to have been born into it. Of course, many of your beliefs you'll want them to imbibe, but what about your limiting ones? I've seen many clients whose phobias were copied from their parents, or who grew up believing the world was a dangerous place, or people weren't to be trusted, because they shared that particular parent reality too often. **Be what you want to see in your kids.**

Installing in them an optimistic belief system is like vaccinating them against misery. Nothing is more likely to keep them from sitting in my chair than this. There was a study done on a group of nuns who, when they first took their vows, wrote about their hopes for their life. Their letters were scored for optimism and pessimism and then checked against their life span. It was found that, at age eighty-five, 90% of the most optimistic were still alive, while only 34% of the pessimists were. And probably still expecting the worst to be just around the corner.

I'm a huge optimist, my wife less so, and it's been instructive to us both about where this simple difference leads us in our interpretations of things. If I look at a blue sky I anticipate a nice day, Bex will wonder how long it will last. There have been occasions when her attention to potential disasters has averted them; pessimism definitely has its place, I just think it should be a small one, visited regularly but not frequently. In the main, it seems to me that it takes the bloom off life's rose more often than it needs to if it's your prevailing orientation; your mindset tends to become one where protection predominates.

Read this:

Opportunityisnowhere

What did you see? There are two choices. Whichever one your mind spotted first could affect your response to life, don't you think?

When something negative happens to a pessimist they tend to hold the three beliefs about it I mentioned earlier in the book. The first is that somehow it's happening to them because of them – it's **personal**. The second is that they feel it's **permanent**, and the third is that it tends to become **pervasive**, a singular event becomes representative of their whole life. Clients come to see me after a life event like redundancy. I listen to them say things like, 'They let me go, I think because the manager didn't like me, and I didn't really fit with what the company wanted. I'm devastated, I gave ten years to that company – who's going to want me now? We'll probably lose the house, the kids are going to hate me because we can't afford to send them on the school skiing holiday, and even my wife is treating me differently. I'm a complete failure.' If you look you can see all three elements of a pessimistic explanatory style present in their story.

Compare that to an optimistic client who comes for coaching. 'I've been made redundant, which is a bit of a blow, but also an opportunity. I could see it coming, the company needs restructuring and my role wasn't a good fit for where they need to go. It's going to take a bit of adjustment from the family but I've got some ideas that could be really good. I'm excited.'

Optimists live longer, are healthier, suffer less from stress and depression and appear to have happier relationships. Teaching ten-year-olds the skills of optimistic thinking cuts the rate of depression in puberty by half.

A major way you can influence this is your explanatory style. Whenever things happen to your children, or to you, especially emotionally charged things, have these three factors in your mind. If they break something and you respond along the lines of 'You're so clumsy!! There's no point having anything nice, you ruin everything!' you're making it personal, permanent and pervasive. Over time, if this is your reflexive explanatory style, you're moulding a pessimistic mindset in your child. This isn't to say you give them a free pass for behaviours you want them to adapt or situations you want them to learn from – if they were playing ball near the vase then more thought could prevent it next time, but explain what you want that event to mean while avoiding the three no-nos. 'These things happen sometimes, but not often if you think for a moment of what could happen. You're a quick learner, I doubt it will happen again.'

If they come home having failed to get into the soccer team and say, 'They didn't want me. I'm rubbish, I'll never be any good,' notice how they've managed to hit all three elements of the pessimistic explanatory style we want them to avoid. If only they could be as accurate with a football. I'm going to talk later in more detail about failure and the mindset required to improve from a setback, but I'll say right now that I don't think it's useful to join in with the vote against them, as in 'Oh well, they know what they're doing, the others are just better than you – you're good at other things.' At this moment these other things don't matter, it's soccer that's the most important thing in your child's life because it's the focus of how they currently feel about themselves. I'd match them in their assessment of their personal ability, then work to make it temporary. 'You may not be good enough *yet*, so we'll just have to figure out what you need to get better at and work at it. Ian Wright wasn't picked by two football teams and look at him' – i.e. it might be about his abilities, but they don't have to be permanent. There's no suggestion it has anything to do with anything other than football. And it's true about Ian Wright. He'd failed at several trials for professional teams and was eventually spotted playing for a Sunday league team by a Crystal Palace scout.

A key component of optimism is hope. The absence of it in my clients is the biggest flag for potential suicide risk. Children tend to be hugely, permanently, hopeful; like my dogs. Each day they sit beneath a tree watching a dove who roosts there, looking down at them in a mocking kind of way (it's a mock turtle dove. Thank you, I'll get my coat). They remain convinced that one day it's going to forget how to sit, and how to fly, and fall in their laps. Children, especially those under seven, are like this, and largely remain so until puberty. Then they lose a lot of it. I wonder if that's a result of us teaching them to be more 'realistic'? Believing, as I do, that we create our own reality, hope seems a useful tool to keep with us throughout life. If we can link being hopeful to taking action, to having the right mindset about failure in the minds of our children, then they'll never give up, always be optimistic about what they can achieve, and be ILOC in their pursuit of it.

Meditating on Mantra 5:

- Get all of the family to write down the positive attributes of everyone else. Have a list for every member and review them as a family on a regular basis. Make it a 'strengths party'.
- Reflect on your recent explanatory style. Are you avoiding the 3 errors of pessimists?

MANTRA 6:

They're not difficult, they're just not you

One of the most fundamental errors in our thinking is that **we assume everyone thinks the same way we do.** In fact, there's a whole range of differences between us, the unique combinations of which go a long way towards describing our individual character. These differences explain a lot about ourselves, and also explain a lot about what drives you nuts about certain other people – your kids included. In my book *Lovebirds* I wrote about couples and the challenges faced in many close relationships. I grouped some of these differences I identified as important ones into eight types, which I named after birds who roughly (very roughly) shared some of these characteristics. I'm going to delve a little further into these character types and the way they interact with the world, adding some extra differences that I think you're going to find amazingly useful when it comes to understanding the person you're raising – because I expect they drive you mad sometimes (and if it's only sometimes you're one of the lucky ones).

The thing is, **they're not you, but it's easy to forget that.** No doubt they have some physical similarities your brain recognises (even if you don't), and over time they're likely to start sharing mannerisms and ways of speaking with you and your partner that unconsciously builds the feeling of familiarity that accompanies similarity. That's just one thing that causes us to forget they are not us. The second is some clever kit we have installed in our brains called mirror neurons. Essentially, every time you see somebody do something, your brain runs a simulation of it. So if someone in front of you scratches their head, your brain imagines you doing it too. Scientists think mirror neurons may be the basis of empathy – if I see you upset, and imagine myself behaving in the same way, it's going to give me an understanding of how you feel, and a clue about how I should respond. Interestingly, people diagnosed with autism and Asperger's have mirror neurons that don't fire properly, leaving them 'blind' to these kinds of social cues. Mirror neurons may also be a major way we learn – by observing and copying others, which is another reason why spending time teaching your children practical skills is so important for bonding.

In terms of your child, it means that whenever you see them do something, or they tell you about something they've done, your brain runs a simulation of it, which is where things can start to go wrong. If my son came from school and said, 'Dad, my teacher told me off today because me and my mates were being too noisy in class. It was so unfair, we were only talking about the lesson,' I'm going to imagine me being him. The mistake is to think that my version of this event and his are the same. Of course they're not, it's just my version of it. How I see myself responding to it will depend on the kind of person I am. If I'm like him, I'm likely to feel the same sense of unfairness. If, however, I'm the kind of person who gets distracted by noise around me and believes that students should sit quietly, then I'm probably going to feel bad for having behaved in this way, and my response to him is probably going to be unsympathetic, and maybe even punitive.

It's key to not only realise that your child is not you but that your child is also not your mini-me, and to understand who they are instead. I'm going to give you some labels to describe certain differences that I hope will really help you understand your child and communicate with him or her more effectively.

One small aside. These descriptions are not intended to pigeonhole anybody. Use them lightly to explain differences and similarities, but please be aware that contexts can affect them, people can change, and if you put someone in a box they often learn to stop looking beyond it.

I'll begin with the types I highlighted in my earlier book, *Lovebirds*, and then add from there. There are many ways to describe the various traits we exhibit; the ones I'm going to be telling you about include ground birds and sky birds, introverts and extroverts, and judgers and perceivers.

Ground birds vs. sky birds

This section describes the difference between people who like detail compared to those who prefer to concentrate on the big picture. In relationships I find it to be the most predictive of discord of all the differences you're going to read about. Have a read through the different descriptions and think about whether you recognise yourself or your children in any of them.

Ground birds

As the name suggests, these people are not given to flights of fancy. They like to know where they are, they like things to be certain, and they are more comfortable the more information they have. They learn sequentially – i.e. they are good at 'working a problem' by moving through it in a planned way, whether it's they who formulated the plan or it was given to them. For that reason, they can be reluctant to go off-piste and explore possibilities. They may even stick to a plan even when it becomes clear to others that it isn't working. The familiar will often be mistaken for safety. They are usually good at organising things, and they like things to be organised. They will accumulate rules about the way things should be done and become attached to them. Their way is often mistaken by them as being the only way.

Sky birds

Possibility is a major attractor for this group. They tend to have a good tolerance for uncertainty because it's in uncertainty that most possibility resides. They can quickly become bored with routine and will always be looking for new ways to do things. The challenge for them is to stick with what they've been told to do – or, more precisely, to do it the way they've been told to. Organisation for them doesn't come naturally because they often have a poor attention span when it comes to detail. Anything mundane can seem life-threatening. For the same reason, rules fall below their radar, particularly those that don't make sense or matter to them. They learn by looking for patterns and relationships between things and are strongly guided by their intuition.

Ground bird children

If you're not a ground bird yourself you might sometimes wonder, looking at your child, who the adult is in the relationship. From an early age, ground bird children can begin to seem very grown up in their desire to organise their lives and the lives around them. They'll be the children who arrange their dolls and toys in particular ways and get upset if they're moved. They'll seek to stipulate the games they play with their friends – and then be heard dictating how the game should be played. Their way will be the right way. Many temper tantrums may result if they feel their rules are being trampled on. The good news is that they'll often be tidy and may even go through stages of being extremely helpful with household tasks. They'll be pretty responsible for a child.

They won't take to change too readily, so moving school can be a trial; a change of a favourite teacher, a trauma; a move of house, the end of the world. You might find they take a while to make their mind up about things, especially where there is a choice. They like to have lots of information on which to base a decision. Which brings me onto detail. They like it. This means that if you ask them something like, 'How was school?' you've probably got to drive home slowly if they're going to be finished with the ins and outs of their day by the time you pull up. It also means that they'll ask you loads of questions about any single thing and can even seem quite obsessive about needing to know.

They learn by steadily accumulating understanding. If there are five steps to get somewhere they'll happily visit each step, even if they've figured out the answer by step three. Steady and solid are probably going to be words you'll hear at a parents' evening. This trait, when found in combination with a passion or interest, can lead to them becoming extremely good at a narrow range of activities – like playing the piano, or a sport, or a particular subject.

You know those girls who have a handbag from the youngest age? Probably a ground bird. There'll be things they like to have with them, just in case. Ground bird children become particular about the way they like things from very early on. They can often have some quite strange fads and fancies going on, from the cup they drink from to the type of cornflake they prefer. Then there's the rules. They like certainty and feel secure when they have it. Rules are a great way of making their world more predictable, if only everyone else would follow them. This can be extremely frustrating for a ground bird child. In their world it's obvious how things should be done but they're only a child so the world doesn't always comply. If you've ever been in a household where the parents seem to suffer from the tyranny of their child's likes and dislikes you're probably observing the consequence of letting a ground bird child rule the roost, and it's often not pretty. When it comes to who is training who, there must be only one winner.

To help them grow, respect their need for order without allowing them control over the way the family operates. Honour their rules whenever you can, but don't let the rules rule them. I talked about the importance of making novelty part of a child's life. This is especially true for ground bird children. Rules give them comfort but can also become a prison. Rather than let them settle in their comfort zone it will be more developmental for them to learn to deal with spontaneity and uncertainty, but be careful to pace it and be ready for tantrums if it's too much. Allow them as much control over their space as you can. Support any drive towards mastering a skill or immersing themselves in a hobby. When they're stressed they'll tend to isolate themselves by dealing alone with what is stressing them. Encourage them to share, to delegate, and to see the bigger picture.

Sky bird children
First and foremost, if you pin your happiness on your sky bird child keeping their room tidy you're going to grow miserable really fast. They just won't. Not because they're dirty and disgusting, or lazy and idle, but because they probably just don't notice the mess. It's not that important

to them. It's a symbol, really, of how they actually thrive on disorder. These children are always exploring, looking for how things fit together, and experimenting with whether things that don't, could. As a result, they're usually highly creative. You can expect them to have mad passions that last a fortnight and cost you a fortune. Their bedroom, and probably your house, will be littered with the equipment and accoutrements that go with what my dad used to call 'five minute wonders'. Don't worry, they'll grow up knowing a fair bit about a lot, and be a whiz at Trivial Pursuit.

They're going to make the loudest fuss about doing things that bore them, that are menial or appear to them to be trivial. They're sky birds, anything that pulls them down to earth will be resisted. They'll come up with the most ridiculous plans and flights of fancy. They will surprise you sometimes by managing to see one through, often with spectacular results.

You're going to need to be patient because they're often late developers. It's not that they don't focus, it's just that their focus is set to a wide beam, not the laser of a ground bird. Their talents often come to the fore when they move into strategic positions, which are mainly higher up the work ladder.

As you'd expect, they're not sticklers for detail, and will struggle to wade through school work which is full of it. For example, in history, dates, lists of people or the political machinery of the Jacobean Parliament will be a major opportunity for a snooze. Get them interested in the patterns of history – about how the conditions of Armistice in 1918 and the composition of the Weimar Republic combined with the fear of another war in the minds of the major European powers created the conditions for Hitler to rise to power, and you'll suddenly have their attention. They love the 'why' of things, so much more than the 'what'. If you ask your sky bird child how their day was you're likely to get an 'Ok' or a 'Boring!' type of answer. Short, sweet, big picture. Extracting more from them can be a bit of a stone squeezing exercise.

Finally, rules. They don't have many. They don't have time for many of other people's rules either.

It might feel sometimes as if they're deliberately ignoring yours. While that prospect exists, it's just as likely that their mind was elsewhere and they simply didn't recognise that now was the moment when your important rule was supposed to come into force. As with tidiness, you'll get old trying to get them to notice. My advice is to pick the house rules that are most important to you. Keep the list fewer than seven. Keep them visible and refer to them whenever there is a breach. With much repetition you might get compliance most of the time, even if not understanding of the need for them.

To help them grow you need a light touch and to play a long game. They're going to find their way. It probably won't be your way. It might take a while. Let them explore what interests them, however transiently. Expose them to as many ideas and directions as you can – they're life's seekers. And, at the same time, build up their tolerance for detail. Help them get better at focusing on the small things that bore them (refer to Mantra 3, especially the Sawyer Effect). They can delegate when they've climbed the ladder; in the early years, learning to sweat the small stuff will accelerate their progress and increase their social flexibility.

So that's the kids, recognise yours? Now on to you, the parents.

Ground bird parents

You are likely to be marvellously attentive to your children and it'll be a rare day when they arrive at school without their PE kit. If you read about ground bird children first then you can probably anticipate some of the things I'm going to be pointing out as things to be aware of. The first has to be your rules. They're going to be important to you and, as you become a parent, having rules and right ways of doing things are going to be a major way you feel in control and that you're doing your best for your child. The thing is, having kids is a messy, chaotic business. It makes sense to try to limit that, but you'll never eliminate it. Do your best to be content with doing your best. Muslims have a saying, 'Perfection is for God'. It's why their art always has a deliberate flaw in it. I'm an atheist and couldn't agree with them more. Perfection doesn't exist, especially when it comes to raising kids.

It might be a useful exercise to sit down and write out all the rules you expect your children to follow, it might surprise you. Rate them on a scale of one to ten regarding how annoyed you would be with a transgression of each one. Ask yourself, would it really matter if you ditched this rule? Children thrive when they know where the boundaries are, but they get constrained and stressed if they're too tight, and present in too many areas of life. **A plant can't grow if it's pot-bound. Neither can a child if it's rule-bound.**

Be aware that believing there's a right way to do things can inhibit your child's creativity. Let them play, make a mess, use the wrong colour crayon, play with the box instead of the present. Take them to fun things, then leave them to find the fun. Don't try to organise the way they have their fun, or point out how you'd be having it. I fully expect a wall chart to make an appearance so the children know when they should do their chores, when the holidays are, and the dates of everything significant to the family. Don't let your life be dictated by it. Allow some spontaneity – and you're not allowed to put a planned spontaneity day on the chart – that's cheating.

If you have a ground bird child they're going to be responsive to the way life with you ticks like a Swiss watch. It will make them feel secure. My big tip is to encourage them to organise themselves, rather than you orchestrate their life. It will grow their resilience and sense of autonomy. There is a danger with a ground bird parent that the child just gives up because what they do is never quite as right, as well-planned or as well-executed as you'd do it. Resist the temptation to take something off them, saying, 'It's quicker if I do it myself!'

Most importantly, if your child is a sky bird don't label

them negatively. It's easy to see them as dreamers, air heads, inconsiderate, and chaos monkeys. They're not really. They're just not you. It's likely that they're going to frustrate you by not living life according to a plan and may seem to be getting nowhere – in your estimation – for quite some time, but trust them. **Even if where they get to is nowhere to you, it might be the right kind of somewhere to them.**

I'll be repeating myself when I talk to the sky bird parents because I think this is an important point. The aim of my describing people by type is merely to enable you to predict certain preferences and use them for a positive effect. It's never to limit them, or think that they're destined to be bad at something simply because it doesn't come naturally or they don't instinctively warm to it. **Children are very plastic, and that is to be encouraged.** Whichever type your child is most like, encourage them to explore the alternative. If they like order and regulation, give them experiences of spontaneity and chaos that turn out to be enjoyable. If they shy away from detail and rules find an activity that has them which is fun – like Brownies or martial arts. Flexibility is a marvellous characteristic we tend to lose as adults. Nurture it in your child and they will find more situations in which to thrive.

Sky bird parents

You find it easier to be the fun parent than the punisher. It can be such hard work to keep your eye on all the things your child 'should' be doing. It often feels hard to sanction them for things you know you'd also fall prey to. You're likely to be great at getting your child to explore stuff – soft play places, new games, different interests. What will come less naturally is maintaining focus on the state of their homework, whether they've got what they need for school, who is actually picking them up tonight. Your mind is usually so full of possibilities that the whirr of life that is a family can easily just become a background noise.

Sky birds tend to have a good capacity to tolerate uncertainty. The upside of this is that you can be happy rolling with things as they happen. I think this is admirable, but then I would, I'm one of you, but pesky research has shown that children like a certain degree of certainty, as evidenced by boundaries, routines and favourite pyjamas. During the process of children's prediction software becoming more accurate, it's no surprise that they use home and their parents as rocks of stability from which to launch into the uncertainty of the world. Be aware of that, and be careful about dropping a casual idea about buying a motorhome and taking the family on an expedition to Peru. I know that it's just an idea. We both know it probably won't happen but it's fun to think about. Your kids may not, so handle your thoughts carefully when you're sharing them.

If your child matches your type you'll have loads of fun exploring different stuff, content for them to pick up and drop interests. There is a bit of a danger that you might apply a bit of unintentional pressure for them to share yours. There is an equal danger that if their interests bore you, you won't spend time with them. Your tolerance for tedium is pretty low, so hire someone to push the swing if you have to. Your child is likely to be very curious. One of the most bonding things you could do is to take the time to explain the world to them, to open their eyes to the wonders of it and to take them places that make them question. In later life, they'll treasure your trips to the museum or the day out at the exhibition of their latest passion, or, when they're older, sharing opinions about politics (or anything). The key is to avoid being certain or prescriptive. Give them permission to think out loud, to float ideas and have opinions without feeling that they risk your disapproval.

If your child is a ground bird you may struggle to connect because their world is so different to yours. The key thing to remember is that more things are important to them than matter to you. Watch and listen for their rules and preferences. Don't belittle your children for having them. It's easy for you to label them as precious, anally retentive, bossy, boring and pedantic. Just don't. They're none of those things, they're just not you. They find comfort in routine and doing things a particular way, just like you find innovating exciting. Flying by the seat of their pants is scary for them. They like clear instructions and believe that there is always a right way to do things. As they get older there is a danger that they'll think their way is the only way, so their teens can be interesting. You probably won't understand why they take the time they do to do something, when you can clearly see the next move. It's their life and they'll live it their way, however much you point at where they should head. And you watch, they'll build something that's theirs.

Just as with the ground bird parents I'm going to encourage you to increase your child's flexibility. The purpose of pointing out a preference they have isn't to limit them with a label, but for you to understand how to use what comes naturally to them, and to avoid differences creating a distance between you. Although they might have a preference for ground bird over sky bird or vice versa, children are incredibly adaptable and it's perfectly possible to make them more flexible in the way they behave by giving them opportunities to practise what lies at the other end of this continuum. Stretching your ground bird by giving them experiences that require them to go with the flow, to improvise, and to let go of the reins, is helping them to grow. To cause your sky bird to have to focus on detail and learn the benefits of rules will help them too. If you can raise a child to be able to move between both preferences, you'll have an adult as comfortable with how things work as how they could work if something changed.

Sight, song, thinking and feeling

At this stage I'm going to divide ground and sky birds into four further categories based on the idea that we have a preference for which sense we pay most attention to. Some children will be sight birds (visual), some song birds (auditory), some feeling birds (kinaesthetic), and some may begin to emerge as what I called thinking birds. I'll come to them last. Once again read through and see if any of these descriptions resonate with you.

Sight bird children

I hope you have a lot of energy. From the moment they open their eyes to the moment they close them sight bird children are likely to be on the go. If you can, connect them to your housing energy supply, it'll cut the bills substantially. From an early age they're probably going to enjoy dressing up, be attracted to shiny things, even begin to have an opinion about what they should wear and how they want their hair to look. If they're a sky bird too, their attention span is going to be fleeting because they'll keep getting distracted by the next favourite thing. Sight birds tend to take things in very quickly, so need a lot of stimulation or they'll get bored. The time you spend with them is likely to be very important. In a way, they measure how much you care about them by how much attention you give them, so they can seem a bit high maintenance. You can't substitute yourself with a video game with these kids.

If they have siblings they might be really tuned to the fairness of what you give each of them, because gifts have a special meaning for them – i.e. they're packets of love. If they perceive their sister or brother is getting more than they are, they'll see it as you expressing a preference, so be ready for tantrums and attention seeking. If there's a situation where one is getting something the other isn't, make sure you explain why. When it's them who is benefiting, point out that this is one of those occasions where their siblings are going without. It might help. A little.

As they get older their own space will become more important to them. They'll want a room, or part of one, which they can make their own. They'll be quite possessive of their own stuff and often find sharing their toys and clothes difficult. It's not that they're selfish, it's just that they fear other people will 'spoil' what they have. In other respects, they'll be as sharing and kind as you make them.

To help them grow give them room to run, literally as well as metaphorically. Being cooped up will drive you both mad, so give them space to burn energy. Open their eyes to the beauty of things – plenty of trips to galleries and museums. Expose them as cheaply as you can to arts and crafts. They're likely to try a lot. The time you spend with them is the same as the gifts they receive, every second counts as love, so if your work makes you suddenly less available to them be ready for tantrums and insecure behaviour, and do your best to make it up to them.

Song bird children

Earplugs. Buy some. You'll go from 'I can't wait to hear their first words' to 'Make her stop' in a matter of months. Song birds live through sound. Musical mobiles are a must, background noise is probably going to comfort them, but not as much as your voice. Once they find theirs they're going to use it to fill every space they're in, silence is not an option. If you put a toy in their cot there's a good chance they'll talk to that for quite a while.

Music might be an early love, and almost certainly a later one, whether just falling in love with a singer or an instrument. Console yourself that if you're listening to an eight-year-old learning the violin or electric guitar at least it means you're not listening to their stream of consciousness. If they're a ground bird, they will never be able to give you a short answer to anything. Sometimes it will seem like telling you about their day at school seems to be taking as long as the day itself. If only patience was a pill. If your child is a sky bird instead, the level of detail might be less but instead you'll be bombarded with their imagination and be expected to join in with it. Often, especially with extrovert song birds, stories aren't just to be read, they're to be acted out with as many voices as you can muster. As they grow up you'll be a sounding board for their ideas and dreams. Let them have them, indulge them where you can, crush as few as possible; their imagination could be their future.

They'll know you love them if you tell them, and potentially only if you tell them. Tell them first and tell them often. Make sure you mean it when you say it because they'll be able to tell the difference. Don't make promises you won't keep. You'll soon discover they're keeping track and can regurgitate the conversation word for word. There is no escape, so be careful what you promise. Also, be mindful of your tone. Song bird children can be hurt deeply by verbal criticism, by sarcasm, by an unkind word – and, like all other words, they won't forget them.

Be prepared for teachers to complain about your child

being disruptive. What it usually means is that they're talking in class. Of course they are, that's how they learn. Good teachers will listen for what they're talking about, bad teachers will just tell them to shut up and listen – i.e. stop learning. Protect them from that.

To help them grow, give them time. Be their sounding board. Give them interesting experiences to talk about, pique their curiosity about the world. Join them in their learning, it's how they learn best. Watch out for an interest in anything verbal or musical and feed it. Make reading to them at night part of their nightly ritual – every parent should, but for song birds it's especially important. Make 'I love you' the last thing they hear every night. In the right tone of voice.

Feeling bird children

Of all the children types, these little people will be the ones for whom a cuddle from their mum or dad is the Holy Grail. They can also seem high maintenance because they're so sensitive to their environment that everything will need to be right. From early on there'll be a preference for what materials they like best next to their skin. They'll cry because they're too hot or too cold. You'll be rocking them too hard or too soft . . . the list may actually prove to be endless. As I remarked in *Lovebirds*, adult feeling birds seem engaged in a lifelong pursuit of sensory perfection, which will migrate from a favourite T-shirt that they'll refuse to stop wearing until it falls off them to an adult fixation with the perfect coffee.

Feeling birds learn by doing and by copying. You may well come into the living room one day to find the television dismantled because their intelligence often lies in the practical. This may cause problems at school, especially after ten years old, because schools don't tend to cater for their style of learning. Once class becomes a sequence of sitting, listening and watching, rather than rolling around and making things, feeling kids can become bored and be labelled as disruptive as they move to the back of the class and start lobbing things at their mates. They often leave school as apparent under-achievers, with a belief that they're not very clever. Actually, what they're not very clever at is being the kind of child that schools are suited for.

Hopefully they'll find their way into a job where their practicality is an asset, like catering, engineering, electronics, and the kind of nursing that involves actually nursing rather than four years of university.

Engaging your child early in physical movement like 'tumble tots' is a great idea. Introducing them to as wide a range of sports and active activities as possible will often lead to them falling in love with something that might last a lifetime.

Above all, nurture their tactility. Physical touch is a vital ingredient of their wellbeing, they'll know they're loved by how often you spontaneously offer a hug, and feel the cold shoulder of your disapproval by the withdrawal of your stroking. Of all the types, they're going to be the last to be too old for a kiss goodnight, which is a pain if they grow up living a long way away from you.

To help them grow, reward their practicality as strongly as you might reward another child's academic prowess. Honour their fads and sensitivities, while not allowing them to become too precious. Nudge them out of their literal comfort zone.

Be aware that they often don't see into the future that well, so how they feel in the moment can easily be mistaken for how they're going to feel for ever, which makes pain, discomfort or unhappiness seem worse for them than others. A hug from you is medicine. Immerse them in the fun of creating things. Do your best to be tolerant of what they destroy in order to learn – they will be very hands-on. Hands on your radio, your watch, your car . . .

Thinking bird children

These are dear to my heart because I'm one of them. I think of them as a sub-set of the other three types because I don't think we're born this way, I believe we learn to be this way. Essentially, thinking birds grow up withdrawing from the world and into their heads. I see a lot of them for therapy. Their issues are usually centred around not feeling as if they belong, a fear of showing or experiencing emotions, and a sense of being disconnected. I find, in these cases, that their childhood included things they didn't like the look, sound or feel of. Not always huge and horrible things, often it was just the drip of disapproval, of disappointment, of not being understood, that was coming from their parents. But I don't think that's the whole story. I believe thinking birds may sometimes just be the result of only children left too much to their own entertainment, or children not being given the opportunity to mix with their peers, of being made to study at the expense of social contact, or a home disruption like divorce or parental strife where their head is simply the only refuge they have.

This makes it sound bad. I've just read through it and almost felt sorry for myself but it's not all negative. It isn't – they can just be quite challenging to get close to. Thinking birds need to make sense of everything so they'll have quite a relentless curiosity about anything that takes their interest – it's rare for them not to be an expert about something. They won't do anything that doesn't make sense to them, they won't get out of bed without a plan, and they'll tend to be quite bad at hiding the fact they think someone is wrong.

They spend a large amount of time in their heads. Even if they're sitting next to you it can feel as if they're miles away. Chances are, they are. There is always a conversation going on in their head. Your job as a parent is to make it a good one, not one about how nobody likes them or how dumb they are. So the messages you send to them are key to whether their inner voice is their best friend or their worst enemy. You can guess which version rings me for an appointment – and where most of the negative dialogue originates. They can seem secretive because they keep their thoughts locked inside and will sometimes think they've said out loud what they've said to you in some internal conversation. As a consequence, there'll be lots of 'But I told you that!' protestations, so don't leap straight to the idea that they're lying.

They tend to do well academically. While you'll worry about the way they seem aloof or distant sometimes, by most measures of life they turn out successfully. Their greater challenge is to be happy. So it's lucky I wrote this book.

Thinking birds emerge during childhood which means that they have another type – sight, sound or feeling – running underneath. A child who is a combination of thinking and feeling birds is often indecisive because they're an equal mixture of head and heart. Knowing which way to jump – between what feels right and what makes most sense – can be a real struggle. They might also be less in tune with their bodies and environment than your average feeling birds.

Thinking bird with sound bird means they're likely to be more talkative and open than most thinking birds, and also more easily put off by people talking around them.

Thinking birds who began as sight birds might disappear with painting materials and not emerge until they've finished a version of the Sistine Chapel in their bedroom.

To help them grow, give them plenty of opportunities to connect with their bodies through sport and other physical activities. Also encourage them to connect emotionally – a pet is a great idea – and to be ok with expressing their feelings. Encourage them by doing it yourself. They often fear that letting in any emotion will lead to being overwhelmed. Teach them otherwise.

Having shown you some of the reasons why differences between you and your children might be the source of some of the challenges you're having, I now want to add another layer of difference that has a major impact on the way we see the world and interact with others. You'll have used these terms many times I'm sure, but I'm going to use them in a particular way.

Introvert and extrovert

What do you like to do at the end of a working day? Go out and socialise with your friends, or retreat to your bath for a quiet read and a good book? When your child gets in from school what do they tend to do? Dump their bag and race out to play with their mates, or sit quietly and watch TV or play a computer game?

In simple terms, and by that I mean my own, extroverts get energy from people whereas introverts lose energy to people. This is a continuum, so people fall anywhere between these two points. As with my previous descriptions, I'm going to be describing the strong elements of each type, trusting you to recognise that you may need to dilute them if you, or your child, fall somewhere between the two.

If you're ever organising a party, extroverts are the people you need to make sure you invite. Firstly, because they're more likely to come than your introvert friends who will moan to themselves about it all day and hope for an excuse to present itself, and secondly, because they'll actually mingle and make some noise when they arrive rather than head straight for the kitchen or whatever shadowy corner is available. Classically, a couple with this as a difference between them will arrive at the party and the extrovert will body-surf into the living room, bounce around all the guests, make new friends, engage with old ones and be the life and soul of the party. The introvert will use their partner's entrance as a distraction while they find a safe spot, scanning the room for anybody they know. If they're not comfortable in the group they'll fade into the wallpaper. And then, some time in the evening, their extrovert partner, who probably hasn't seen them since they came in the door, will find them, take them by the hand and say, 'Come on, come and have a good time.' What they mean is, 'Come and have my good time.'

This misunderstanding of each other's needs can extend to parents and children. Extrovert children need a lot of stimulation because they get bored quickly. Having people around them is an absolute requirement for them to thrive. They are likely to be noisy, boisterous and outgoing. They'll make friends with anyone and wander off in the supermarket if they see something that looks interesting – especially other people. As they get older they'll spend a lot of time with their friends or communicating with them. Even getting them to stop texting at the dinner table is going to be a big ask. When it comes to study there is little point locking them away in their rooms until they've done their homework. Let them do it at the kitchen table, or Skype their friends while they're doing it, or have a study-buddy round. Silence for them is not conducive to anything. Make sure if you get them a phone, and if you're paying the bill, that they have unlimited free texts and a strict limit on how long they're on it, otherwise their bill and your mortgage are going to look very similar.

An introvert child, on the other hand, is much better at amusing themselves. They will probably disappear into their bedroom for hours and play happily with just their toys and their imagination. Their attention span is good. They will often become keen on a hobby or interest that they'll pursue with a quiet passion. They make friends more slowly than extroverts, and their circle of friends is likely to be quite small. A necessary quality of an intro-vert's friend is not to demand their regular attention; they might love you to death, and be prepared to donate their kidney to you, but only actually feel the need to see or speak with you three or four times a year. When it comes to study they will need to withdraw into a quiet place. The worst of all activities will be group work. Until they're comfortable with a group they'll be loath to speak up in front of it. In fact, where extroverts are quite happy to speak their thoughts out loud even if they haven't thought them through, introverts will be much more private and only offer something when they're sure of it. When I teach, I always offer the opportunity for questions – and encourage the group by saying the only stupid question is the one you don't ask. Extroverts will happily raise their hands and ask something that tests that idea, whereas many introverts will wait until the break, when I'm bursting for a pee, to creep up and say, 'There was just one thing I was wondering . . .'

In the past, I've heard parents exasperatedly point out other children to their kids and say, 'Why can't you be like those other children?' What they're usually pointing at is junior versions of themselves. Introvert parents will like children who are quiet, self-motivated, and who don't make a fuss. Extrovert parents will like (and expect) their children to be boisterous and noisy, run in a pack, and create a bit of mayhem. Their usual response to a moment of reflection in their children is to say, 'You're very quiet, what's wrong?' It is vital that you let them follow their nature, not conform to yours. I see clients who've been labelled as shy their whole lives, when all they actually were was an introvert in an extrovert household. In addition to being called shy and boring, stick-in-the-muds and wallflowers are other common labels they tie around their kids' ankles.

I've also seen clients who were told they were show-offs, big-headed know-it-alls who needed to be in the spotlight. Clients who've grown up scared to show their potential. You've guessed it, extroverts raised by introvert parents. At school, introvert teachers who don't understand this important difference are going to label their extrovert charges as disruptive and disobedient – and even suggest they have Attention Deficit Disorder. Extrovert teachers will decide that their introvert pupils aren't showing enough interest or interacting enough with their peers. Guess who gets made to stand up and answer questions in front of the class to help bring them out of their shells? Guess how many of them come to see me as adults with a fear of speaking in front of people?

A final pair of distinctions, and ones which, if they're a difference between you and someone close to you, are going to produce fireworks . . .

Judgers and Perceivers

Judgers like to get to the end of things, to get closure, to be done with stuff. Give them a deadline and they won't be happy unless they beat it. Perceivers like openness, possibilities and options. Give them a deadline and they'll start negotiating for an extension. I've literally had to prise exam papers out of Perceivers' fingers because to hand it over closes the door to the possibility of what their result could be if they had just a bit more time.

If this is a difference between you and your kids you've got some work ahead of you. Imagine a Judger/Perceiver couple out shopping. This is what you'd hear from the Judger, 'I can't believe you've had us traipsing around town for hours looking in every bloody shop for something we saw in the first one we went in!' Sound familiar?

For Judgers, time is connected to manners. 'I'd rather be an hour early than a minute late' is an adage of theirs. For a Perceiver, 'I don't know where the time went' is the most common greeting they'll find themselves uttering, seemingly without any awareness of the impact their lateness might have on others. If you're late for a meeting with a Judger they'll see it as rudeness, if you're on time for a Perceiver they won't be ready.

Both Judgers and Perceivers could go backpacking around the world, but whereas a Judger would set off with a detailed itinerary, knowing exactly where they were going to stay for a good period ahead, what to do when they got there, and what the names of all the cabin crew were on each flight, the Perceiver would turn up with an open ticket, probably miss their first plane but not seem to care, stay at each place for a random period of time, and arrive back home within six months of their expected date thinking they'd kept to a pretty tight schedule.

If you're a Perceiver parent to a Judger child the best description I can give is by analogy. If you watched the TV series *Absolutely Fabulous*, and remember the relationship between the mother, Edwina, and her daughter, Saffy (Saffron), you will look a lot like them to outsiders, with a child who does more organising of you than you of them. It's likely that the older they get the more they'll shake their heads in disbelief at *your* life choices, while you won't understand why they don't lighten up and smell the roses more. As you can see, the negative labels are likely to fly here. From one direction will come the accusation that you're rude, inconsiderate, inconsistent, unreliable, and an airhead. From the other will come the opinion that you're a narrow, obsessive, and unforgiving control freak. It'll make for some interesting dinner table conversations – if the Perceiver turns up.

Understanding difference as a parent

The key benefit I want you to get from having read this section is this idea that we are all different and that these are some of the ways we can describe those differences. I want them to be a language that opens up your joint behaviour, attitudes and beliefs to a conversation between you that doesn't degenerate into name calling and slamming doors. **Your children have reasons for doing things the way they do them; they're just not your reasons.** I've found it very freeing to see my children's behaviour through the lens of these types because it stops the urge I have to make it about them as a person. It reminds me that the way I see the world is only one choice and one version of that world. To expect my children – or anyone else – to align with that version seems both ludicrous and wrong. Spending time looking at the world through alternative eyes keeps you young. Which is useful when so much of what your kids do feels like it prematurely ages you. It's all about balance.

A big lesson I learned as a parent (and I wish I'd learned it a lot sooner) was that rather than wish my kids were more like I wanted them to be, I needed to think about what kind of parent they'd like *me* to be. We'd all be great parents to ourselves, but **who does our child need us to be for them to grow and thrive?** It's a question that never loses its relevance, no matter how old they get. It's about how to get the best from them, not how to get the easiest ride as a parent for you. And, strangely enough, by doing it, your ride will get easier.

It's not just the differences between you and your child that will help. Knowing the types of everyone living in your house including partners, grandparents, or whomever your unique family is made up of, will provide a rich vein of understanding about the difficulties that people living together inevitably creates. Knowing that your partner is a ground bird and you a sky bird will help you understand why they seem so hard on the kids compared to you (in your eyes). They're not being hard, they just have different ideas about how things need to be achieved (but notice how easy it is for the negative words to creep in). By the same token, just because you're not remembering to get them to tick their homework off on the wall planner it doesn't mean you don't care. It's just a difference. Talk about it. If you're an extrovert it doesn't mean your partner isn't committed to the kids because they don't want to help you coach the swimming team or fund-raise for the PTA. Making the sandwiches or building them a website is contributing too. Having a child who never seems to open up to you doesn't mean you're failing as a parent, or that they don't love you − they may just be a thinking bird. Don't suggest they're somehow odd, or they'll come into my clinic in twenty years telling me they feel like they're somehow odd. If your kid's idea of a great day isn't getting muddy, they might just be a sight bird who likes to look shiny at all times. If they can't even let you have a bath in peace without telling you something else about their day through the door, they're probably a sound bird. If it doesn't matter to you that your underwear is synthetic plaid, but it does to your daughter, chances are she's a feeling bird, and you're probably a thinker.

So often, the people who sit in front of me seeking help have nothing wrong with them, per se, other than what they've been led to believe about themselves as a result of the labels their parents gave them. Those parents didn't mean to harm them, the very opposite in fact. They were trying to get their children to adapt their behaviour in ways the parent thought would make them safer and happier – i.e. be more like them. It's the hardest thing to remember that our kids aren't remote-controlled toys. Doing things their way works for them. It's our job to guide them towards becoming better at guiding themselves. In order to do that we have to understand their guidance system, not try and get them to function with ours.

Meditating on Mantra 6:

This is a lifelong meditation. At least it has been for me.

Whenever someone is doing something that is annoying or frustrating you, or just seems bonkers, ask yourself:

'How is what that person is doing about a personality difference between us, rather than about them as a person?'

Remember, where your children are concerned, your grandchildren will be your revenge.

Growing ILOC children takes bravery

Fighters, flighters and freezers

My proposition in this book is that our protection response has been a big gun in the armoury of our evolution, keeping us safe from predators and other assorted physical threats for millions of years. However, it is now working against us by getting called into action in response to threats our brains perceive to our self-esteem. I say working against us because it isn't just ill-suited to this task, it's actually counter-productive. The protection system reduces our ability to think clearly during the time it's in operation. It reduces the control we can consciously exert over our behaviour. In a modern world, when we most need our wits about us, those very wits are disappearing over the horizon with an imaginary tiger at their heels.

There's nothing better to save you from things with sharp pointy teeth, but nothing much worse to protect you from the criticism of your boss, the potential ridicule of an audience, or the disappointment of a partner.

I've described how our culture isn't helping. Advertisers use our lack of self-esteem to sell us products we're told will boost it. The media focuses on the worst of human nature as entertainment. Disaster and ill-fortune as the main features of our news. Perhaps our governments foster an atmosphere of threat to keep us convinced we need their leaderships. All these external factors mean that many of us are triggered into a state of protection more often than we need to be. And then there are our parents.

The point of this book is to get you thinking of two very simple calculations when you're with your children, **'Are they in growth or unnecessary protection?'** and **'Is my parenting contributing to them becoming ILOC or ELOC?'** Our children's brains become tuned to what they're used to. The more they perceive themselves to live in a world where protection is necessary, the more they'll find evidence for needing that protection in the world and from the people around them. They'll learn to assume risk and threat in everything and everybody (what the thinker thinks . . .). They'll live a life in protection, which increases health risks, reduces their possible choices, and limits the things they dare to do with their lives.

If, however, they're tuned to see the world as a place to grow in, their bodies experience less stress, they anticipate fewer constraints on their choices, and they can pursue their potential. If they're told they're stubborn and difficult from the day they're born, then they become tuned to respond to other people in a way that will be markedly different than if they're identified as being flexible and laid back instead. The words their parents use to describe them can come to define them – and be the difference between whether they struggle within their image of themselves or are raised free to decide for themselves who they are.

If our experiences lead us to live as a person who lives mainly in protection, the kind of person we tend to be falls into three categories which mirror the responses the protection system evolved to keep us safe. If I wheel out the sabre-toothed tiger one more time, what has our brain found to be the best responses to it charging at us with lunch on its mind? We can either fight it, flee from it, or freeze and hope it doesn't see us. Individually, we'll tend to favour one of these over the others. Let me use three clients as models: Sharon, Kevin and Louise. Each comes to see me for confidence issues. Imagine all three describe the same childhood incident when I regress them to find the Significant Emotional Event they believe is at the root of their low self-esteem. I'll let Sharon describe it:

'I'm about eight years old and at home with my mum. I want her to play with me, but my baby brother isn't very well so she doesn't have the time. It feels like she never has time now he's here, she's always playing with him. When she says no, I shout at her and she smacks me.'

So far so similar, a classic occasion where a child can evaluate the situation from its singular position and conclude that she's not totally loved, or loved less than someone else. It's a chink in her previously held belief that she sits at the centre of her parent's universe. At this point the responses between the three clients diverge.

Sharon tells me, 'I run to my brother's bedroom and smash one of his toys.'

Kevin says, 'I just can't move. All I can see is my mum's angry face looming over me. I think I close my eyes and shrink inside until she goes away.'

Louise tells me, 'She looks so angry, I'm terrified. I run away and hide under my bed.'

All three children come to the conclusion that they're not as loved as their siblings. What I've found is, in the people who go on to become my clients, the butterfly effect links it to further occasions their brain finds similar. This leads to doubts which have an impact on their belief about what other people think of them. They generalise not being loved by their mother to doubting they're lovable to anyone. If this memory gets matched to a future event in front of a group it can lead to a fear of public speaking. If it gets matched to peers then you can get an adult who finds it hard to make friends. If it gets matched to other people in close relationships then you might have someone who fears rejection in their relationships. It's why I love my job so much; every client is a puzzle, where a chain of events that their brain decided had a relationship to each other causes them to become a version of themselves which includes a limitation. During our sessions the plasticity of the brain allows us to unravel the tangled strings of misinterpretations that comprise the puzzle. We then pick the knots out of it, leaving the client free to live without whatever used to hold them back.

Anyway, back to the plot. With each of my clients this

reflexive response could become the way they behave whenever they feel threatened. If Sharon's boss criticises her, she's likely to throw her toys out of the pram and react aggressively – if only verbally. If Kevin's boss does the same he'll probably stand with his mouth working like a goldfish and only think later of what he could have said in his defence. And Louise? Possibly run to the toilet, possibly go sick with stress, possibly start hiding her work to avoid any further censure.

If their event-chain connects to relationships then Sharon is likely to be possessive and jealous. She'll shout and scream if she thinks her partner has looked at someone else, or cut up his suits if he works late with that new secretary. It's likely that, when she meets someone new, she'll sabotage it by getting her rejection in first. The moment she feels intimacy is growing she'll do something to drive him away, often by pushing him to prove his commitment. Usually she ends up testing the relationship to its death.

Kevin will be the classic guy who spots someone he fancies, can't hold eye contact, gets tongue-tied and confines himself to wistful looks from a distance. If he somehow manages to get into a relationship – usually with someone who pursues him – there's a danger that he'll become a doormat, unable to stand up for himself and doing anything for a quiet life.

Louise? She'll turn dates down, find excuses not to meet anyone, put obstacles in the way of any suitor. She's so scared of being hurt that she hurts herself by keeping at a safe distance from love.

To stop parents panicking – and this may be a few paragraphs too late – I want to stress that I'm not saying that every moment of inattention from you, any slip in your language, any moment of preference you show to one child over another, is sentencing your precious offspring to a life of misery. These events tend to just be peaks, surrounded by the foothills of other similar moments. In other words, they represent an attitude over time, a conclusion about how a parent felt about them. If you communicate your love to them (in ways *they* recognise, remember) without strings or conditions, they'll be ok. Not perfect, but ok, which is all anybody can do for their child. Growing them secure in your love will mean that when you have those moments of annoyance, exasperation and frustration, those moments when you wonder why you bothered, when you do or say something you later regret, you won't have to worry that your shortcomings are going to be sobbed out in my chair twenty years hence. Raise them resilient, raise them ILOC, raise them loved, and your failings won't matter against the backdrop of that success.

We all need a protection system. Your kids will have moments in their lives when some physical threat will be posed to them – from a car accident, to an incident in a pub when they're out with their mates, to a dog threatening them in a park, to a bully threatening them in a playground. With each of us having a preference for whether we tend to fight, flight or freeze, it's a little bit of a lottery whether it will be the best response in the situation they face at the time. I find it quite a sobering thought that I'm only here because my ancestors' preference happened to fit whatever threats they faced, while many millions of others perished because theirs didn't.

When you look at the training people in the army, or police or fire service receive, you'll recognise that much of it is to overcome their natural instincts. As an ex-police officer there were many occasions when I had to walk towards what the public were moving away from. There were many times when I felt the urge to run, to freeze and to fight. If I succumb to my urge to fight aggression with aggression, I know I'm going to stand in court in front of a chubby face in a fancy wig accusing me of using excessive force. If I run, I let down the uniform, my mates and the public. And if I freeze, well, same thing really. So training helped to damp down these survival responses and keep me consciously in control. The shakes came afterwards.

In young children, a lot of what they decide is threatening comes from your response to it. A case in point is my grandson Heath. We have a lovely miniature Schnauzer called Fred who has issues – the irony of that in a therapist's pet is not lost on us. Heath was eighteen months old and loved to walk around the house. For some strange reason Fred felt threatened by him – maybe it was the staccato, random motion of a toddler, who knows? His reaction was to run at Heath, barking. I confess, while I don't think he'd ever bite, and he always pulled up short, my heart was in my mouth each time he did it. Not so my sensible daughter-in-law, Tara. Seeing Heath jump and look at her for a reaction, she just nonchalantly said, 'Is Fred talking to you? Tell him Sssshhhhhh!!' and wagged a finger at Fred. Within a few repetitions of this Heath simply responded with a stern finger and a very cute 'Ssssshhhh!!' and Fred retreated looking miffed. At an early age Heath is already learning to treat his reactions as choices, not things he has to obey. It's not about drilling the natural and instinctive response out of them. It's about training them to stay in control of their actions. It's about teaching them choice. And often that will involve you being brave.

Similarly, when they're older and you notice them fighting, flighting or freezing in social situations, the opportunity exists to sit and coach them through their choices. Here are some questions that can help them reflect and redirect their behaviour.

1. When you have an experience you want to change, what does it most feel like,
   a) An urge to fight, or get angry or defensive?
   b) A feeling of being frozen, tongue tied or difficulty finding words?
   c) An urge to run or in some way distance yourself from what's happening?
4. If this was happening because of something you're scared of, what would that be?
5. If it was your friend who felt this way what would you say to them?
6. Think of someone you respect. If they watched you in this situation what would they say that would help?
7. Think for a moment of what you would look like in that

situation if you behaved how you'd like to. Pay particular attention to your breathing, to your posture. Rehearse that feeling in your body until you can find it when you want it. ('Who would you be if . . .?)

You can also teach them a fantastic little technique for managing their feelings. It's called spinning and it's for those moments when you get a feeling you don't want.

Spinning

1. Notice the feeling. If you could point to where in your body you're feeling it, where would you point?
2. If you could imagine that feeling as a shape in front of you, what shape would it be?
3. If that shape had a colour, what colour would it be?
4. As you pay attention to that shape, imagine it rotating. What direction is it going?
5. What happens if you spin it faster, does the feeling get stronger? (For most people it will. We do this to show that people have control of their feelings. They're usually more open to the idea of being able to make things worse than make things better. If it gets weaker, great, it's what we wanted.)
6. Now slow it back down to where it was so you can see that you have control over it.
7. Now make it go even slower. And slower and slower. Slower until it stops, and when you notice it has, notice

what else has happened. To your breathing, and to the feeling.

With a bit of practice people are able to regulate their emotions using this technique very quickly. The more confidence they have in their ability to do this, the less often they get the feeling. By taking action they learn they're not slaves of their emotions. To make it even easier I've recorded a download to guide you or your child through the process. Go to www.questinstitute.co.uk/growresources

Meditating on Mantra 7:

Fight, flight and freeze can all be appropriate responses in the right circumstances; what's important is improving your choice. If you think your child is developing a default response, encourage them to retain control by putting them in similar situations but with a lower fear/anxiety quotient. Afterwards, sit and talk through what they did and what they could do next time, emphasising that it's about a behaviour, not their personality. Teach them spinning so they have the means to control their emotions in the moment.

MANTRA 8:

Don't expect

I've mentioned Gil Boyne several times now. He was the only hypnotherapist to be trained by Fritz Perls, the father of Gestalt therapy. One of the things Boyne took from Perls was what is known as the Gestalt Prayer, which therapists get clients to repeat after they've done particular sessions, usually involving the re-evaluation of their childhood relationship to one or both parents.

Part of it comes in the form of two statements. The first they say in relation to their parent(s),

'I am not put on this earth to live up to your expectations of me.'

Think about this for a moment in relation to your own parents. Think about how maybe some of your life has been driven by trying to live up to the hopes your parents had for you – whether clearly stated or covertly delivered. If I apply it to myself, I can see quite clearly that I joined the police mainly seeking validation from my dad. I was an academic kid from a family with very set working-class values. I was the first to go to grammar school and get A levels, so I was considered a bit of an oddity. I wanted to study philosophy at university. It wasn't received well.

I left school and got a job in a publishing company against ninety other applicants. My dad's response, in his joking kind of way, was to dub me a 'shiny-arsed pen pusher'. My brother had left school at sixteen to join the police cadets and seemed to me to be viewed immediately as a success. Looking back now, I'm pretty sure I joined the police to beat my brother and rise a little in my father's eyes by doing so. My unconscious plan succeeded in that I got promoted ahead of him, but failed in changing what I thought was my dad's opinion of me. And it set me in a career direction that took me eighteen years to change because I was so stuck in ELOC.

I haven't shared this with you to blame my dad, his opinion of me was mainly in my head – what the Thinker thinks rules – but rather to get you to nod at how some of your life direction may have been motivated by input from your parents – including what you made their input mean. I also wanted to highlight how my dad was just passing on some of his childhood to me. He came from a very working-class family. When he left the RAF he ended up driving lorries for a living before making the huge switch to selling cars. It wasn't an easy transition with four children to support, but he persisted despite being put under pressure to 'stick with what you know' by family members close to him. Interestingly, while he became successful and moved into truck sales, he never aspired to management. It was, perhaps, too much of a step in one generation.

The ironic thing is, however, that when it came to me, his pressure mimicked that which was applied to him, and for the same reason – to nudge me in the direction his own past had taught him was safe. I choose to believe that all behaviour has a positive intention, even when it causes a negative outcome. I see this as a prime example. I also see it very often in my clients and friends, and I've felt the pressure of it myself when in the role of parent. While it was ok for me to leave a secure job and strike out as a self-employed hypnotherapist, when it comes to my children I feel my protection system urging me to get them to make safe career choices, especially now Heath, Sasha and Seth are with us. So it was, I see now, with my dad. Out of love for me, he unconsciously pushed against me leaving my roots, while attempting it himself. And the way he often did it, with sarcasm and unkind nicknames? Well, his family had a strong theme of men being strong and rough with each other. I learned later that his dad called him names which my dad interpreted as signs of affection. In lieu of being able to openly express feelings, such roughness is quite common among men – I saw it a lot in the police – it's just that my young self didn't recognise it as that at the time. It was unfortunate that what my dad interpreted as affection from his father, I interpreted as meaning the opposite. I spent years trying to live up to what I thought was his expectation of me. I believe that people are doing the best they can with what they've got. Sometimes our parents lacked what they needed to communicate their love, or the intention behind their actions, clearly enough to us.

When I realised this, the old story I told myself about not being good enough in my dad's eyes simply disappeared from my head.

I'm hoping that sharing this with you has caused you to nod at some of your motivations for some of your life decisions – and has maybe provided a catalyst to begin to change those you're unhappy with. I also hope it might help you understand how easy it is to seek growth for yourself, but unconsciously keep your children in protection. Good parenting requires bravery.

If my story hasn't resonated you should probably treat your parents to something; they've done a good job of not transmitting their expectations of you to you, or making your worth dependent on your choices aligning with theirs. Anyway, that's enough about me. Back to Gil and his two statements.

The first was,

'I am not put on this earth to live up to your expectations of me.'

When the work has been done with my clients I find they make this statement about their parents quite easily. They can feel a massive weight lift from their shoulders as a result. It's usually the second statement that proves harder to say – and mean. Again, it's to the parents:

'You are not put on this earth to live up to my expectations of you.'

Hold the phone . . . so my parents don't have to put up with my crap, don't always have to drop everything to help deal with my latest life crisis, shouldn't have to put their plans on hold to help me out financially? They have a right to their own fears and insecurities? Are you sure? I'm certain I saw it in the contract?

Most of you reading this will have been lucky enough to have parents who you continue to be able to count on. Sure, they have their foibles, but you have little doubt of their support. Just take a moment to consider that. If you let go of your expectations of them, how much freer would *they* be? If you couldn't count on them how much more would you appreciate them?

Look at the two questions and place yourself in the generational cascade.

Your children are not put on this earth to live up to your expectations of them.

If you read that quickly I expect you nodded in agreement, but read it again. Do you really agree with it? After all, you've worked very hard so far to raise them. You've made endless sacrifices and bent your life into a new shape to accommodate them. Shouldn't you have some expectation of being able to enjoy their ride through life a little – and some right, given your life experience, to exert some influence over the route they take? Yes. You should have some expectation. No, you have no right to it. And it's really hard to separate the two.

Our brains are designed to have expectations for us, if they weren't we wouldn't know the meaning of disappointment. You know now about mirror neurons. When we think of our children's choices we can't but help to run simulations of them, and from that derive an opinion about what their best choice is. That is the error we make. You are not your child. The brain they will use to make their choices with is not the one you just used to run a simulation of their situation. The resources they have, the way they see the world and the things they have that you don't – and don't have that you do – means their simulation will be different. They can't live their life your way, and neither should they.

It doesn't mean that you shouldn't advise them. Here is what I say when my clients ask for my advice, 'I'll give you my opinion, but not so you'll follow it, just as something that might make you see something useful to you. What you do with it is your responsibility.'

I use that word *responsibility* as a deliberate reminder of our goal as a parent – to grow an ILOC child who listens to the opinion of everyone they value – sometimes even people they don't – and then make their choice and own it. Which leads to the second statement:

You are not put on this earth to live up to your children's expectations of you.

There comes a time in a child's life when it's good for you to 'let them down'. Watch birds and their chicks. The parents work tirelessly to bring them worms and grubs, to clean their nest of the chick's detritus, and to encourage them to fledge – to find that they can leave the nest under their own steam. Most bird species continue to feed their young for a while after fledging, but do so near the site of the food. Many times, I've watched chicks who are mere inches from the bird feeders in my garden flap their wings and demand their mothers transfer the seed to their mouths. That soon gets old. There comes a time when the parents leave them to it. The chicks, no doubt complaining that it's *so unfair*, start feeding themselves.

I have some clients who come to me still flapping their wings. They complain about how their parents don't understand how difficult their life is, how unsupportive they are, how critical they are – as evidenced by the refusal to pay for the child's latest life crisis. Such clients usually project the parent role on to the world at large – their boss is unfair and demanding, life generally is so hard, the universe never gives them a break. They sit, and flap, and plead with me, the latest in a line of parent-figures.

It's inevitable that our children have expectations of us that are, largely, so taken for granted that they're invisible to them. After all, you have spent probably nearly twenty years fulfilling a role as provider, protector and scraped-knee-kisser. There will be times throughout your kids' lives when it might be appropriate for you to return temporarily to that role in the face of a life crisis, but to return to the role means you have to have left it. How can you expect your children to thrive in the world if you've always protected them, provided for them, and soothed their every bump? The process of parenting throughout their first twenty years is to incrementally shift the onus of responsibility for those duties on to them, not treat those roles as unchanging and inviolable, otherwise you're going to still be doing their washing and cooking when they're thirty, paying for everything when you go out with them, and ringing their boss to ask them why your little poppet hasn't been promoted yet.

The best way to release yourself from the tyranny of your children's expectations is to increasingly withdraw yourself from them as the years go by. Teach them that they get in relation to what they give – with money especially. Teach them how to protect themselves by raising them to be ILOC. Teach them to welcome bruises as a learning opportunity. It means you'll have an adult relationship with your adult children, not a groundhog day life of living first to fulfil their needs. As an aside, I think one of the steps to true adulthood is to knock our parents off their pedestal as Mum and Dad, and recognise them as Harold and Hilda. I don't mean call them by their first names, that is still considered by some people to be weird, I mean see them as people. Sometimes something can occur that makes this happen. My parents divorced when I was twenty-one. I had already left home, so it wasn't that big a deal in most selfish respects, but it did cause one major shift – my parents became human. From these icons that the words mum and dad tend to represent they suddenly became mortals: sometimes scared, sometimes stupid, sometimes fallible. I lost something in the process, but I think it was worth it. I've seen quite a few clients who never let their relationship with their parents grow up with them. Mum and Dad remained people to lean and rely on, to follow, and try to impress. Many suffer terribly when they lose one or both of them, often unable to move on in their life for years afterwards. Make an effort to meet your parents as fellow grown-ups, it's a major step towards ILOC. As your children come into their twenties encourage them to do the same.

Remember always, **you weren't born to only be parents.** The area of your life that falls outside this label is every bit as important to your wellbeing and fulfilment. You simply can't exist solely as Mum or Dad, or your children's expectations of you will lead to you having expectations of them. You end up in a co-dependent relationship that grows nobody.

I have parents who come to see me – mothers especially. Almost exclusively, if I'm honest. Exclusively, if I'm being *really* honest. They talk to me of having lost the meaning to their lives. They feel depressed and empty. Their kids have left home. They spent so many years meeting the expectations of their children and letting those aspects of themselves that weren't 'mum' wither away, that the only value they felt they had was from that role. They pour so much of themselves into motherhood they're left empty. You've heard it called *empty nest syndrome*. If you're a mum reading this, or a dad for whom this applies, keep your life as 'not mum' or 'not dad' as a vital part of your existence. Not only could your life be enriched when it's time for your kids to fly but so will the subsequent relationship you have with them – where they tell you of their adventures in the world (because you've raised them ILOC enough to be having them), and you have some of your own to share. It seems a part of this modern tyranny of 'perfect parenting' that our identities should be subsumed, that being Dad and Mum should always trump being Dick or Harriet. Create a balance between them and one will refresh the other. Become simply a parent and you're likely to become exhausted, depressed, and lose the vital sense of you as a person.

Meditating on Mantra 8:

Ask yourself these questions and see what comes out. If you take your time – and are really honest – it might get a bit uncomfortable.

- What expectations do you think your parents had of you?
- When you look at your life, how do you think it's been influenced by them?
- What do you still do that is because you feel it's what your parents would want or approve of?
- Are you passing on these to your children?
- How?
- What expectations do you have of your children?
- How do you communicate these to them?
- Having read this far, is this what you truly want to do?

If not, what can you do differently instead?

PART IV:
GROWING THROUGH
THE AGES

I was a little reluctant to have a section dividing childhood into stages because I'm not an expert in child development, but there are things that I've learned that can be particularly relevant to certain timeframes. While I've said that you'll get most value from the book if you've read it in its entirety, and that's true to this point, this part of the book is certainly where many of you will just want to dip into the bits most relevant to you. Feel free.

Growing through the ages

Pregnancy

Start before the beginning

One of the earliest influences you can have on your child is by taking steps to maximise the positive feelings you experience as a mother during pregnancy. I know that isn't always going to be easy. Sometimes it's going to be impossible, but over the course of the nine months, if you create opportunities to deliberately stimulate the parasympathetic system – that part of you that releases the hormones connected to relaxation and calm – it could reap dividends. You might find you experience a trickle-down benefit from just ten minutes of deliberate relaxation that lasts throughout the day and takes the edge off of anything that would otherwise make you tense.

During her pregnancy Heath's mother, Tara, was taught a number of techniques to help her relax and visualise a positive connection to her baby. Such states produce positive hormones – endorphins. How much better to let your child's brain soak in those for nine months rather than in stress hormones – how much more likely is your baby to anticipate a positive world when it arrives if that's what its brain is most used to responding to? Heath was the calmest baby I've ever met. It might be that we've simply lucked in as a result of his genes, but I think the emotional state of the mother, and the content of her blood, played a big part.

I am a huge fan of teaching mothers simple relaxation and visualisation techniques. I've recorded a download specially for all my pregnant readers (or readers who know anyone pregnant) to enable you to develop the skill of achieving calmness by design and create whatever would, for you, be the best possible connection to your unborn child, so they can spend nine months surrounded by your love. I can't prove that such things work, I only have scores of women who've sworn that it has. If you'd like to download it simply go to www.questinstitute.co.uk/ growresources. The password is chelseaforever, just because I want Arsenal fans to have sleepless nights.

So, that's your mind playing its part in giving your baby the best time in the womb you can without installing a merry-go-round. I'm not going to talk about diet because that's not my area. Suffice to say that you're building your baby out of what you eat. If you flood their bloodstream with sugar because of a craving for chocolate, don't cry about how wired your baby is when you're lying awake all night. It's a sad thing that some babies need to be put on drips to wean them off the sugar addiction their mother has unwittingly given them. **The womb is the first chance to help your child towards growth as a state of brain.** Take it.

But let me reassure you. The womb is only the *first* place to tune your child towards growth. Stress (and consuming bucket loads of chocolate) can be an inevitable part of pregnancy and if yours has been particularly difficult there is no point adding to that by beating yourself up about it. Children's brains are incredibly plastic, so how they are at birth doesn't consign them to an inevitable future. There are many things you can do to nudge your child towards a more relaxed way of seeing the world now that they've arrived. I'm confident that if you follow the philosophy of this book, and exemplify it yourself, your child's brain will adapt positively, whatever its time in the womb was like. It's never too late to change a mind.

Anchoring

Would it be useful to create a positive response in your child that you can cause every time you give them a particular stimulus? Actually, wouldn't it be handy for you too? Such a thing exists. It's called 'anchoring' and it's based on the tried and trusted principle of Pavlovian responses. You may have heard the saying 'Neurons that fire together wire together'. It basically suggests that if two things happen at the same time they can become associated together. An everyday example of anchoring are traffic lights. You might be daydreaming as you drive your car, but if the light turns to red your foot will move to brake – sometimes even if you're in the passenger seat. Advertisers spend millions trying to 'anchor' their brand to a product. If you're a certain age you'll remember what Beanz meanz?

A successful association like this means that unconsciously, as we browse the baked bean shelf, we're likely to notice Heinz beans first. If you have to watch adverts, notice how many are basically exercises in anchor creation.

There have been several studies showing that children respond to music in the womb, and also, that listening to Baroque music – most commonly Mozart – can boost learning. Put the two things together and you now have 'Mozart for genius babies' products. I don't know if they work, but I do think we can utilise music as an anchor.

For our purposes, if you play music to your baby while she's in the womb, especially when she's quiet, there's a good chance she'll associate that music with all the lovely comfort of the womb, including the connection to Mum. When she's born, if you play the music as you put her to sleep, 'firing' the anchor at this point could reproduce in her these associations and she may settle faster. The more you use an anchor in this way the more powerful it becomes. Use any soothing music that you like. If you find the evidence about Mozart compelling, then why not pick a piece of his?

There'll be lots of things you can anchor in your child in order to trigger them into positive responses to things. Children use them quite naturally – like having a teddy to comfort them (and doesn't it explain the fuss they usually make if they lose it?). Here's a cautionary tale about anchoring, though. When my mum was potty training me, she'd encourage me to sit by going through a book with me. Obviously this had a strong effect on me, because to this day I can't go into a book shop and browse without having a strong urge for . . . well, you know. So, just put some thought about the consequences further down the line of the anchors you create. Was that oversharing?

0–7 years

Now they're here, what next?
With the pregnancy taken care of (how much of a typical man did that make me sound?), what to do when they're born to give them the best chance in life?

There's been a huge surge in hothousing babies' IQs, as if IQ is the best predictor of a happy, or even a successful, life. I mentioned the Mozart products. They're only one part of an industry that seeks to persuade you that they can help get your child into university by the time they're out of nappies. Here's the thing; we want our children to be successful, in my opinion, because we think successful equals safe. Good job, nice house, security. I see loads of clients who are successful by that measure, and they're coming to me because they're unhappy. Why are they unhappy? Because they don't like themselves. They fear others don't like them either, they're scared they're not good enough, that they'll be rejected, that only perfect is good enough. Sometimes they're scared that they're stupid, despite all the evidence in the world that it's not true. If you're reading this, a low IQ probably isn't the thing to worry about. Defining success as living a life that is happy and fulfilling is the goal I'm setting this book. It is the goal

I want to help you achieve for you and your children – independent of your specific aspirations for them or you.

When it comes to your children, what you do in the first year of their life, and the four or five that follow it, is going to be key in helping them create a life like that. Enrolling them in a mini-Einstein course isn't high on the must-do-to achieve-that list. Lots of socialising with other children, lots of outdoor activity, and a minimum of TV is.

Lots of strokes, folks

This book is about raising children to be resilient, active, open, happy, secure adults. It's about training their brains to see the world as a place of growth, not of unnecessary protection. The beginning of that process is to make them feel secure. Did you know that simply stroking a premature baby for fifteen minutes each day for ten days will lead to an earlier hospital discharge, an increased body weight compared to infants who aren't stroked, and about £7000 less in terms of health costs? Get stroking.

It's been discovered through experiments on rats that the young who are licked and groomed the most grow up to be the most resilient to stress – and they even know why. The grooming turns on the part of the rat's genome which is responsible for controlling the part of the brain that processes stress hormones in adulthood. The effect of attentive parenting is felt all the way down to our DNA and can negate a lot of negative environmental circumstances. A scientist called Blair found that classic contexts for raising disturbed children, such as family discord, over crowding and poverty, only had an effect on a child's stress levels if they had an unresponsive or inattentive mother. If the parenting was good these factors seemed to become irrelevant. When The Beatles sang 'Love is All You Need' they were on to something. In the first year of life, don't worry about 'spoiling' your child with too much attention. The more secure they feel during the first twelve months, the less attention they'll need later – which is when nudging them gently towards independence should probably begin. If they're still demanding to share your bed when they're two or three you haven't achieved that step yet. It may be an indicator that they're not yet primed for growth. Encouraging them towards being okay without you might begin to occupy your attention more.

However, that's for later, for now the first twelve months is straightforward, if not simple. Make eye contact, a lot. Make your face expressive because babies respond more to faces which are. Stroke them, hold them, carry them. Respond to their cries until you've learned the difference between the ones that are designed to control you and the ones that are a request for a need to be fulfilled. Here's another thing I believe but can't prove (science generally doesn't believe memories from this young can be recalled): I've regressed many clients back to memories of being alone in a cot feeling abandoned and not loved; however, only ones that represented a pattern of such treatment were interpreted that way, not occasions where they were just left to see if they'd settle back down and responded to if they didn't. Don't worry that experimenting in that way is going to damage them irrevocably but leaving them screaming for hours might, and picking them up every time they murmur is training them in a pattern of responding to their every whim that you'll still be trying to get out of when they're in their forties (remember who is training whom).

It used to be thought that memories could only be recalled after the time a part of the brain called the hippocampus comes on line, which is typically around age four. It's now been shown that children can respond to things they experienced in the womb, like music that's played to them, so clearly some kind of memory is working long before then. I accept that the idea of accessing it is contentious. Nevertheless, I have to report that many of my clients have. I don't think their memories from this period are like video recordings of the event; I think they're more like interpretations of how they felt, turned into a film. Most of the really early life event recollections that clients felt had led to their problems as adults are to do with the feeling of not being wanted, or not being loved, and the absence of the parent. So my advice is keep them with you, hold them, touch them, talk to them, engage emotionally through your tone and expression. I don't think you need them in your bed – but it's your choice – just make sure you're in a position to respond to their needs. If you think it sounds like the kind of rearing practices that are followed in cultures many in the West consider 'primitive', you'd be right.

Mind your language
From the very beginning, be aware of how you describe your child. While some traits and characteristics seem to

be genetic, overwhelmingly **you grow the child into what they become,** and the first seven years are critical. If you describe them negatively from the beginning – as fractious, difficult, stubborn, naughty or bad – this will alter your attitude towards them, without you even realising it. There's a model called the behaviour cycle. It suggests that your attitude adapts your behaviour, and your behaviour adapts my attitude, which adapts my behaviour.

The Behaviour Cycle

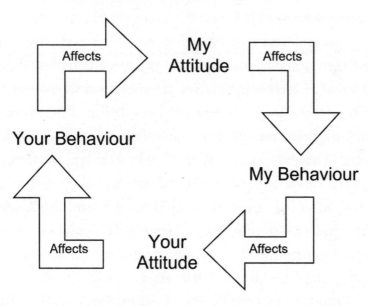

Your baby is hyper-sensitive to your attitude towards her. Call the baby what you want her to become and it will affect the way you interpret her actions. If Hannibal Lecter hadn't been called a naughty boy by his mum it might all have turned out very differently. In Cognitive Hypnotherapy we work on the basis that **all behaviour has a purpose.** Adopt that mindset with your baby so you remain curious about what lies behind their behaviour. It will help you avoid giving your baby negative labels aimed at their character or personality. In the main, what they're doing when they're crying, or unable to settle, or being 'difficult', is expressing a need. When you think about it they have very few ways of explaining that to you. Look for environmental, developmental and dietary reasons for their challenging behaviour before you start labelling your child as difficult, stubborn or wilful.

Keep them moving

When I watch Heath, in his early months, it's easy to mistake his jerky movements for randomness. It's anything but. Every movement he makes refines the next, every attempt to grab an object improves his aim. He's a learning machine. I remember when Heath visited for Christmas when he was fourteen months old – he giggled at my theatrical attempts to catch a tangerine he threw in my general direction. When his dad joined the game he altered his aim and included us both. That's pretty impressive after only 530 days on the planet. In our youth our ability to absorb new patterns of movement is at its most plastic. As we get older we tend to have a more fixed repertoire, which is why we all end up embarrassing our children by dancing *our* way to *their* songs. The more a child is engaged in developing the skill of learning to move, the more likely she or he is to develop an aptitude in physical activities. There's a reason the Chinese start their gymnasts at three, why the children of good footballers seem to enter the professional game more than their friends, and why deciding to take up a sport in your twenties in order to make a living at it is probably a lost cause. The more you stimulate your child's use of their body from the very beginning, from giving them things to reach for, to giving them the chance to stand, to tumbletots to kiddie yoga, to rough and tumble on the floor with Mum, Dad, or the dog, the more likely she is to grow into a coordinated, physically capable adult. Andre Agassi's dad put a tennis ball on a piece of string above his bed as a mobile so he was tracking the motion of a ball from his earliest moments. Just saying.

The key thing to remember is that the skill needs to be something they enjoy. How many children have been put off any physical activity by being forced to participate in their parent's favourite sport, or by the PE teacher's pet punishment? After the pain of running cross country in the cold of winter over the Kent downs aged eleven, I didn't run for fun again until I was forty – and then only to impress Bex. Guess how that went.

Making movement a fun and normal part of their daily life – and children need very little encouragement – can build it into the fabric of their way of life to a point where physical activity is unquestioned. It has massive health benefits, as well as the ability to boost thinking. Twenty minutes' vigorous exercise before a test has been shown to improve results, and people with a history of fitness suffer significantly less from Alzheimers in later life. In the States, an approach called New PE, which rewards effort rather than skill, increases the enjoyment of those children who are less gifted at sports. In the early years, competition is the last thing games and exercise should be about; they should be another avenue for fun, just the kind that leaves kids sweaty – and blissfully tired come bedtime.

In 2011, the antidepressant Zoloft was prescribed 37 million times, yet research has shown that exercise is more effective. Encouraging my clients to get back in touch with movement is one of the first things I do when they present with low moods. On the basis that an ounce of prevention is better than a pound of cure (I tried converting it to metric, but the old version sounds better), how good an idea does it sound to inoculate your child from depression from the beginning just by making exercise a part of their daily life?

Dexterity is a form of exercise too. Taking the time with your child to help them handle objects and tools, having the patience to let them fix things rather than take something off them because you could do it faster, is a parental skill to be prized. I've had a number of male clients who had impatient fathers who didn't take the time to let their sons 'help' them with their interests – from car mechanics, to showing them how to grow vegetables, to letting them hang out in their home gym while they worked out. As a result they grew up with a range of limiting beliefs – about their practical abilities, their manhood, or their likeability. Learning at an early age how to wield a screwdriver is good training for their brain, but what they learn in those moments when a parent is passing on something of their own skills is bonding gold that helps to boost a child's self-esteem enormously.

It's all good...or bad

One of the important things to remember with a child of this age is that they can only see the world in black and white; things are either right or wrong, good or bad. You either win a race, or you lose it. This is called *nominal processing*. Keep this in mind before you launch into long explanations about how it's not the winning, it's the taking part that's important – it will do nothing to stem their tears. Later they develop the ability to be more nuanced, to appreciate shades of grey, but early on keep moral issues simple, and be content with reasonably stark boundaries. Children have been shown to be happier when they're given clear guidance about what is 'right' behaviour, and what is not. The more exceptions and inconsistencies there are, the more they're likely to be confused.

7-12 years

The Jesuits say 'Give me the boy until he is seven, and I will give you the man'. I agree, kind of. It certainly seems to be true that beyond seven your influence on them increasingly takes a back seat to the opinions of their peers, but I see that more as a shift in your role rather than any sense that your job is done. It's just that you're going to have to influence them in a less direct kind of way. Hopefully, to this point, your parenting has been focusing on developing an ILOC mindset, so the ground work has been laid. Now, we want to make sure it becomes consolidated into a habitual way of seeing the world, even though they're going to look to their friends for a lot of their ideas about what is cool. By seven they should be secure in your love for them, which is why as their world expands – it becomes the esteem of their peers that they fear losing.

It's all in the mindset

One of the key factors in raising a child who is successful at life is *mindset*. I want to begin by asking you a question about your talent, or intelligence, or worth. Do you think it's fixed? Do you think you're born with a certain amount of brains or stardust and that's it? If you do, this is called a *fixed* mindset. Or do you believe that nothing is fixed? That you can become more intelligent, increase your talent over time, develop yourself? Do you believe we're made more than born? If that's the case you have a *growth* mindset.

While watching *Match of the Day* I saw this in action. Two of the soccer pundits, Alan Hansen and Alan Shearer, were discussing the merits of an Arsenal player called Theo Walcott. I can't recall it verbatim, but the gist was:

Alan Hansen: 'The trouble is he just doesn't have a football brain. You've either got it or you haven't.'

Alan Shearer: 'I disagree. I think you can see him maturing and making better choices with his passes compared to last year.'

Who would you want as your mentor?

As a parent, consider your belief about mindset. The one you want to instil in your child is the growth one. Having a fixed mindset makes you more concerned about how you'll be judged – which is clearly ELOC. A growth mindset puts the focus on what can be improved.

In the face of failure, a fixed person is more likely to make it about them – 'I'm not good enough' – while a person with a growth mindset will just conclude that 'I'm not growing'. Their response to that is more likely to be an increase in effort because failure is seen as an opportunity to learn more. Fixed people see effort as a negative – 'If I was truly talented I wouldn't have to try this hard.'

Here are some responses to feedback depending on the mindset you have:

Fixed	Growth
'There's no point, I'm giving up.'	'If I work harder I'm bound to improve.'
'I can't change, it's just who I am.'	'I can always be more than I am today.'
'I'm rubbish.'	'I'm a work in progress. I can change.'
'The feedback made me angry!'	'I mustn't shoot the message. What can I learn here?'
'I'm really embarrassed by my failure.'	'That which doesn't kill me makes me stronger.'

A study in the States showed that the most consistent predictor of success at college wasn't IQ, it was grit, sheer persistence. I've seen this with my graduate students. A lot of talented therapists have left our school intent on building a successful practice. Over the years the defining quality that predicts how they'll do is their consistency, how persistent they are at simply turning up and doing something more than nothing to build their business. A growth mindset is the thing that drives such perseverance.

Interestingly, persistence as a trait is evident in children as young as four years old. When being shown something, children who had a fixed mindset only paid attention when they were being told if the answer was right or wrong; they showed no interest when given information that could help them to learn. Fixed children tend to thrive when things are safely within their capability. If things get too challenging – when they don't feel talented or smart – they lose interest. On the flip side, growth children actually get *more* excited when things get more difficult. The process of becoming better is actually better than the feeling of having mastered something. When they feel they have, they often move on to something new.

Fixed people have higher rates of depression, and, as you'd expect, a higher rate of drop-out from college, or any career path or sport they begin. As the famous coach John Wooden remarked, '**You aren't a failure until you start to blame. You can learn from your mistakes until you deny them.**' This is what fixed children do, they blame themselves, or deny they've failed.

Probably the single best book I've come across demonstrating the plastic nature of our potential is *Outliers*, by Malcolm Gladwell. In it he dismisses the notion of born genius. He demonstrates with examples ranging from Mozart to Bill Gates that the single biggest factor in the development of genius is effort. It takes 10,000 hours, the research suggests, to build a genius level skill set. You don't put that much effort in if you believe your talent is fixed by your star sign. Michelangelo once moaned, 'If people knew how hard I worked to get my mastery, it wouldn't seem so wonderful at all.'

Sometimes it must have made him hit the ceiling. I don't suppose it was any easier for the other Ninja Turtles, either.

Unfortunately, this is another thing that runs contrary to our culture and which you'll have to protect your child from. As Gladwell points out, '**Our society values natural effortless accomplishment over achievement through effort.**' The media show us examples of overnight success, and encourage kids to audition for *Britain's Got Talent* when all they have is a desire to have the attention owning that talent would bring. Foster in your child the idea that they can always improve, that failure is part of success, and that their improvement is in their hands. The resulting resilience will protect them their whole lives.

Attributing any success that your child achieves to something fixed or innate, like saying 'You got a 100% in your test, you're so clever,' or 'Jane always does well because she's so bright' or 'I can see Martin turning professional, he's got a God-given talent' actually reduces their effort. If kids pick up the idea that their success is due to a fixed capability they feel less need to strive. Instead, **attribute your children's success to their application**. In terms of cause and effect, make **effort** the **cause** of their **success**. 'You got 100% in your test? Well done, you really deserve it with the effort you put in', or, 'Jane always does well because she really perseveres', or 'I can see Martin turning professional, you should see the work he puts in'.

I have an opinion that **genius isn't a thing you are, it's a thing you have**. Every child has a genius for something. Help them find what that something is, and then encourage them to feed it.

If you can encourage a growth mindset by teaching your children to find the opportunity in any challenge or setback, to believe there's no failure only feedback, by developing in them an intrinsic motivation, making ILOC a habit of mind, and building in them the discipline of actioning small positive habits every day, you're going to create a young person who is resilient, self-reliant, and capable of making his life be anything he chooses.

Watch their language

This is a good age to be using your language to guide the building of their reality and listening to correct anything of theirs that could prime them for protection. They'll be lacing their conversations with statements about themselves, about the world, about everything. This will be true throughout their youth, but this age range is when their brains are developing the capability of a more nuanced understanding of the world, so it's prime for influence. So listen carefully. Sometimes a child stomping away from you shouting 'You never have time for me!' is signposting something significant in their memory. Many of them will be so obviously causal in construction that, with practice, they'll leap out at you:

'Roger never asks me out to play because he thinks I'm stupid.'

'If I wasn't such a nerd I might stand a chance of getting picked for football.'

The list will be endless. Listen for their use of the word *because*, the verb *to make* – as in 'she made me angry when she said that,' or 'Mum makes me feel bad every time she says I'm stupid', and 'If x happens . . . then y results'.

Once you train yourself to hear them, they'll pop up all over the shop. Your job is to contest the validity of your children's negative causations; if they're left to repeat them they eventually become truths. Respond with something along the lines of:

'If it's not that Roger thinks you're stupid, what other reason could there be?'

'Knowing that you're not stupid, what is it about Roger that makes him need to think that about you?'

Listen to the causative statements you make yourself, because those based on your own limiting beliefs could infect your child. Guide them towards positive cause and effect connections:

'That lady saved a place for me in the queue. That was kind.'
'I won at golf today. All my hard work is paying off.'
'My boss was horrible to me today, I don't think he's in a good place at the moment.'

Interestingly, if you listen to the causal statements you find yourself making about yourself, and think, 'Would I want my child to say the same thing in the same situation?' you quickly identify what your brain is using to build this version of yourself. If you then ask, 'What would I like to hear them say instead?' it can begin to train your brain towards a growth path, instead of moving you deeper into the habit of thinking in protection mode.

Give your children good and valid reasons for what you ask of them – 'I'd like you to help around the house today *because* I don't have the time to do it on my own.' 'You can't have a new phone *because* we need to save for a car, and we can't afford everything.'

One of the most important things with causation is to avoid linking things you don't like your children doing – or their shortcomings – with their identity:

'You failed because you're lazy.'
'You're fat because you're greedy.'

In the same spirit, don't suggest to them that other people's limitations are something to do with the person either:

'The waitress brought me the wrong drink, she's stupid.'
'Susan turned me down because she's mean.'

They will learn to look for cause where you point, so be careful with your finger.

Also, guide them towards growth with the questions you ask them. Rather than 'How was school today?' ask them:

- 'Who did you help?' 'Who helped you?'
- 'Who were you kind to?'
- 'Who was kind to you?'
- 'What could you teach me that you learned today?'
- 'What was the most fun you had?'
- 'Who/what made you laugh?' Who did you make laugh?'
- 'What was the hardest thing?' 'How did you cope with it?'
- 'How might you cope if it happens again?'

12 to adult

Aah, the delight of teenagedom beckons. A key thing to remember is that it will end. And much of it really isn't their fault. Research has shown that they really do need more sleep – their bodies are going through an amazing amount of change. Bear in mind that the brain doesn't come on line in its entirety until you're about twenty, sometimes even older, and the last part of the brain to come to life is the part that deals with focus and consequences. It explains a lot, including why your teenager might seem oblivious to the impact of not studying hard enough in the run-up to their exams. When you rant at them, 'Don't you realise what failing your exams will mean to your future?' No, they don't. Their brain doesn't yet have what it needs to work out consequences. No wonder we shake our heads at the actions they take whose negative outcomes seem obvious. No wonder we find it so easy to mock their wide-eyed surprise when something stupid turns out badly. Who thought it a good idea to give them some of the biggest decisions of their lives to make, like what they want to do for a career, when they can't see beyond next Thursday? Who decided taking hugely consequential exams in multiple subjects was a corker when the examinee's brain hasn't yet learned to focus? And in the middle of all this pressure, the body drops gallons of sex hormones into their systems, while our culture is busy telling them they'll never have sex unless they follow an increasing number of rules about what to wear, who to listen to, what product to gel your hair with, and what body shape is acceptable. It might just be that I'm far enough away from my son's teenage years to have calmed down a little, but writing that actually made me feel sorry for them. Being a teenager IS tough.

You might be lucky and have a child who progresses through this stage without a blip or a grouch. If you are that lucky, pretend otherwise to parents who aren't if you want to stay popular. In the normal run of things, you are probably going to have some blips and may even feel like you're losing them. This is probably a sign of good parenting – they're secure enough to fledge and are stretching their wings. Give them as much freedom as you can manage (remember ILOC takes bravery) without surrendering your quality of life. Believe that they'll come back to you. They will. You have their inheritance. Be aware that your influence probably won't count as much as peer pressure, so do your best to avoid situations where they have to choose. Pick your battles wisely. Most mistakes they make probably won't matter in the long run and some things you see as mistakes might actually lead to something great further down the line. The wonder of life is we never know what is going to lead to what, so my main advice is to chill. Increasingly, through this stage, good parenting is giving advice and accepting when it's ignored. If you've raised them in ILOC, you've done the best you can. They will have to own their choices.

Crucially, I want to remind you of one of the mantras. *They're not who they're going to be yet.* I've been a parent for thirty years, and the worry that goes with it hasn't gone away, it's just changed its target. And you know what? It's nearly all been wasted energy. My kids are great – and they're still not who they're going to be yet. I have parents ringing asking me to see their children with things ranging from they're not joining in properly to they're not focusing on their exams, or they're worrying about their spots. I'm not saying that there aren't children who need the kind of help I provide but most don't. Most childhood worries work themselves out and actually provide the turbulence that helps children learn to swim more strongly through life's waters. I was scared of many things as a child – the dark being a standard – and I got through them without a counsellor. If you're reading this your genes are Olympic champions at surviving – they must be strong or they would be where the genes of countless millions of non-survivors are. **Most people who go through trauma aren't traumatised by it.** That's a fact.

In the spirit of letting your children go, of trusting them to fail, and to find growth where you might see danger, I'd like to share with you something my dog Betty taught me, and which I shared in a blog.

The path we travel is ours alone

We live on the edge of Thetford forest, an ancient area once the home – and rumoured to be the site of the grave – of Boudicca. On a misty autumn day, it is easy to imagine hordes of Celts emerging from the trees. It's a great place to let our two dogs run. Fred and Betty differ in their response to freedom just as much as human siblings tend to. Fred will disappear for brief periods in pursuit of Betty but return bursting with excitement at his daring, while Betty simply disappears – often for many long minutes, completely immune to our calling, whistling or promises of treats. She loves to follow scent trails, beyond anything else, and we reconciled ourselves long ago to the possibility that we might one day lose her to an accident or angry stag. But it doesn't stop us getting anxious when she goes beyond her average period of being 'lost'.

It occurred to me the other day, while holding my breath waiting for her to reappear, that the word 'lost' simply doesn't apply to her situation. With my limited senses Betty is lost to me once she is gone from sight in the tree-line or beyond the sound of her breathing. But I doubt that we are ever lost to her. With her amazing sense of smell and hearing I suspect she is always aware of our location, and the trees are a complete irrelevance. I realised that, if I imagined the trees gone, I'd probably always be able to see her, and that her path would be a series of wide arcs, with us as a point on that arc that she returns to periodically to check that **we** haven't got lost.

Maybe it hasn't been so different with my children. When they left home I worried about their ability to navigate life without my wisdom to guide them. Often, from my observation point, they seemed lost. I now realise they were just following an arc I couldn't see – and, like Betty, that arc is a search for what *they* are looking for, not for what *I* want them to find. They always knew where I was if they needed me, and, like Betty, periodically they'd return.

I realise now our children aren't lost because they're not following our path through the forest. They're not lost just because you can't understand the choices they're responding to. Often the trees I imagine them wandering in exist only in my head – to them life might appear a beach, or a wide-open space. What I've found is that, with my boys now thirty-one and thirty-three, their arcs have led them to build their own lives, each quite different, yet both very much their own creation. Not only are they good lives, their journey has made them into men I'm more proud of than if they'd simply stuck to a path I might have chosen for them.

It's not our place to choose our children's arc, as much as our instincts yearn to. Our job is to equip our kids with the tools of travel, love them enough that we remain a point of return, and let them run. To paraphrase singer James Morrison, they're not lost, just undiscovered – especially to themselves. Isn't that act of self-discovery what life's about? As much as a parent I'd like to shout, 'It's over there!' it probably wouldn't be for them. Show them the world, let them run, and remember to breathe. They'll be fine, and they'll bring home some wonderful things. Unlike Betty – last week it was a pigeon.

Only later into writing this did I realise that this metaphor applies to me as well. I thought I was sharing a learning I'd taken from my boys that might resonate with other parents, but now I realise it probably has a personal application to most of us regardless of whether we are parents or not. I spent a long time on a path marked through a forest subtly signposted by my parents, with my best interests at heart, and lit by my society. As I look back now I realise I was more lost on a well-defined route than I've ever been since I left it. When I finally abandoned it for my own arc, propelled by my own scent trail that I absolutely had to follow, I found happiness, fulfilment and like-minded people following their own trails. And my arc was opposed. I realise now that fellow-travellers on the forest path would have seen my swerve into the trees as a mistake in my orienteering – who leaves a secure job only seven years from a pension? I was about to include my parents in that lack of understanding when a memory suddenly came back to me: on the day I left the police I got a card from my mum wishing me luck and expressing her faith. She didn't understand my detour, but she didn't try to tug on my leash either.

When it comes to our own lives I think it's important to be aware of the choices we're making and why. What others on the well-travelled path saw as a detour was actually the beginning of my real direction. My journey up until then had been a detour. Necessary in so many ways, and easily mistaken for the real thing, but a detour nonetheless.

You have to be ready for the fact that nobody else but you may understand your choices – until you meet others following *their* arc. To paraphrase the author Hugh Macleod, the more original your life choices, the less good advice people will be able to give you. So, if you have a scent in your nostrils that irresistibly stirs your blood, ignore everybody. If you're like Betty you won't have to, your ears won't be listening anyway. That invisible scent your children are following could be to the life *they're* here to live. That trail *you* feel drawn to could lead to the same thing. My advice is, take a deep breath . . . and run.

A letter to young people: Seven things I want you to know

Now I admit, this is a bit of a writer's contrivance. Do I really expect your children to read this – especially if you ask them to? Who knows, I'm sure some will, and if it finds its way into their ears from your mouth, that would be great to. I was hugely helped by the wisdom and faith of my grandfather, Fred Cook, and I've no doubt some of what I'm about to share originated with him. I hope it helps you and your children also.

Dear Heath, Sasha and Seth,

1. Bad things are going to happen to you
2. You feed what you focus on
3. Sometimes your fears don't matter, or aren't even yours
4. You get the future you expect
5. Nobody is worth knowing who thinks what you wear matters
6. Sometimes what others try to teach you is because of their own stuff

7. You're writing your life story. Be that character in it you want to be

1. Bad things are going to happen to you

There are going to be days when you'll sit somewhere and cry about how bad life is, how unfair it is, and how much other people suck. It's ok to cry – it's actually a good way to reduce your feelings, and everybody needs a cry once in a while. It's what you do next that's important. Life isn't fair, doing good things doesn't make good things happen (it's just good to do them anyway), and people can only let you down if you place an expectation on them. I believe that life is what we decide it is, and our imagination is a powerful weapon to help us. So I like to act as if bad things have to happen to make good things happen later – and as a result they seem to. I like to act as if I've been given everything I need to cope with what happens to me. And I find I can, even if it's really hard. Acting 'as if' there are good things about you that help you do good things is fine, and way better than acting 'as if' there are bad things about you that stop you doing good things. Like acting 'as if' you're not good enough or nobody likes you.

My granddad told me, '**It's not meant to be easy, just possible.**' And it is, whatever *it* is, if you give what you want everything you have. **You can't negotiate with success, you either give it what it wants, or it goes to someone else.**

Trust me, what life throws at you makes you stronger,

you just won't feel it at the time. In many old cultures they made young boys go through rites that turned them into men. Very often it involved pain – the Cheyenne made boys cut their chests and feed ropes through the gashes, which were then tied to a post. They had to pull themselves free. If you join the cubs or brownies they make you sing 'Ging Gang Goolie'. It's much the same thing. The idea with these old rituals is that out of your pain comes your genius; **out of your wound comes the thing that will reveal your talent.** I've found that you can make this true if you think it is and act as if it is.

What may seem a disaster at the time might actually lead to something good. Just as what might seem a bit of good fortune sometimes leads to something horrible. I saw a worm struggling across a hot patio once. To help it I picked it up and put it on the grass. A blackbird saw the movement and came and ate it. It reminds me of a story I've always liked, also about a Native American:

There was a warrior who had a fine stallion. Everyone said how lucky he was to have such a horse. 'Maybe,' he said. One day the stallion ran off. The people said the warrior was unlucky. 'Maybe,' he said. The next day the stallion returned, leading a string of fine ponies. The people said it was very lucky. 'Maybe,' the warrior said. Later, the warrior's son was thrown from one of the ponies and broke his leg. The people said it was unlucky. 'Maybe,' the warrior said. The next week, the chief led a war party against another tribe. Many young men were killed. But, because of his broken leg, the warrior's son was left behind, and so was spared. The people said it was lucky.

'Maybe,' the warrior said.

You can never tell at the time if things are for the good or the bad in the long run, so enjoy the good bits to the maximum, and don't treat bad things too seriously, and especially not as permanent – there's always the other side of both the good times and the bad. One thing you can be sure of is that nothing lasts, and there's nothing we can do about that, so don't get too attached to things. Suck the marrow from the good times, and plough through the bad without stopping at the 'it's not fair' hotel, or 'the world's against me' B&B.

If you're moving, you'll fall. All that matters is what you learn so you don't fall the same way twice. All that matters is what you find as a reason to get back up.

2. You feed what you focus on

It isn't what happens to you, it's what you make of it. I know that sounds trite, but it's true if you live to its principle. In the film *The Best Exotic Marigold Hotel* someone says, **'Everything will be all right in the end... if it's not all right then it's not yet the end.'** I think that's true, and it helps me enormously.

What is it with me and Native American stories? I don't know, Sioux me, because here's another one:

One evening, an old Cherokee told his grandson about a battle that goes on inside people. He said, 'My son, the battle is between two wolves inside us all. One is Fear: it is anger, envy, jealousy, sorrow, regret, greed, arrogance, self-pity, guilt, resentment, inferiority, lies, false pride, superiority and ego. The other is Love: it is joy, peace, hope, serenity, humility, kindness, benevolence, empathy, generosity, truth, compassion and faith.' The grandson thought for a while and then asked his grandfather, 'Which wolf wins?' The old Cherokee simply replied, 'The one you feed the most.'

If you focus on the bad things that happen, you'll tune your brain to bring more of its kind to your attention. If I say to you, 'Don't think of a blue tree,' what comes to your mind? The brain has to process a negative, so focus on what you want, not on what you don't. Focus on everything good in your day, every day you can remember to do it. By feeding the good things with your attention they grow – and so do you. Every night before you go to sleep, look back on your day and think of three good things in it. They don't have to be big things – I saw my first butterfly of the year this morning – but make them mostly about people or nature. It's even better if you write them down. You'll know it's become a habit when you have to choose your three from lots of choices.

3. Sometimes your fears don't matter, or aren't even yours

When I was a police officer I was often frightened of being thought of as scared because most of my colleagues seemed much braver than me. Now I've come to realise that courage isn't the absence of fear, it's continuing to act despite being scared – and that most people are fighting as hard as you to appear brave to others. So don't be scared of fear, and remember it comes in two flavours. One is the fear of something physically hurtful happening to you. When it comes to this type of fear, a good rule of thumb is that if everyone else is scared (or would be in your position) then so should you be, so act accordingly (from an ILOC position though, you still have power over your response). If that isn't the case, you're in a situation where you have a choice. Focus on what your head tells you and follow that.

The second flavour is the fear of other people's opinions. When it comes to this type, let me share with you the biggest learning of my whole life: **there is no more fun you can have in your life than simply being yourself.** That's it. Have fun being you and most of the things you fear disappear. If you worry about what others think of you, you twist yourself into whatever version of you you think people want to see, in each situation you find yourself. So many people come to see me with an identity crisis – they say they don't know who the 'real them' is. It's because they have too many versions to choose from as a result of their need to suit other people. Just be you because everybody else is taken. How can anyone get to truly know you – and love you – unless you show them 'you', and the best way to do that is to have fun being that person. People will find you much more attractive because it gives them permission to let the pretence go from their side too. You can spot people who are comfortable being themselves because they're usually laughing more than most, and doing things they enjoy for themselves, not to impress or go along with others.

Sometimes people hear me say this and think it's a recipe for selfishness – permission to have fun doing what suits them and hang the rest. I don't think you'll find that – if you're really 'you'. I believe that **kindness, giving and service to others are the most natural behaviours of people in growth.** A lot of the fun you'll have being you will be to do with those things.

Then there are other people's fears. When you're young, some of these fears will be those of your parents. They love you, and I've discovered that the biggest fears I carry are for my children – and now my grandchildren. Our fears can cause us to act towards you in a way how we wouldn't act with others. We'll sometimes try to stop you doing something because of the fear we have of something happening to you. Let me tell you a scary story. When Sasha's dad was sixteen he said he wanted a moped. I didn't want him to, but I had one at his age, so how could I say no? I put the obstacle in his way that I thought would stop him – he had to buy it himself because so had I. I now realise my parents probably set me the same condition for the same reason. Against my expectation, Stuart did it. I think I bought his helmet to make sure it was a good one. On the big day, I took him to pick it up and then followed him home. I dry heaved in the footwell inside a mile, so scared was I by how bad a rider his inexperience made him. That's the fear your parents have when they say *no* to you about some things. They're making up a picture in their head of what might go wrong if you do what you're asking for. So understand it, forgive it (remember that they're learning how to be parents as you grow up, so everything is new to them too), and sometimes when you're older, ignore it – but be prepared to take the consequences. You can't live inside a bubble of other people's fear, or it becomes your reality. I know your parents are going to let you do lots of things that scare them. Good. You probably need to do a few more than that. I trust you to know which ones, because if you break your leg don't come running to me. Just make sure you do it because you're having fun being you, not to impress or please others. And don't rebel against your parents' wishes just because they're their wishes. Rebelling against *everything* isn't really rebellion, it's just another type of conformity.

The last type of fears are the fears other people try to pass on to us. They do this in a number of ways. The most common, and the one to be most aware of, is the fear of not being good enough, of not being liked or loved. Some people will try to make themselves feel better about themselves by making you feel worse. **Always remember that people can't take your power, you can only give it away.**

So don't. If you feel hurt by someone else's comment, ask yourself, 'What is it about them that makes them need to say that?' You'll soon find the answers that come to you reveal the insecurities of others. Practise this. It's a brilliant protection from other people's attempts to contaminate you with their feelings about themselves. Remember that unkindness to others isn't strength, it's a red flag for that person's own vulnerability. Remember **if people are trying to make you feel weaker it must be because you're stronger.** You'll find that if you're just having fun being you, truly you, kindness will come easily, and so will an invulnerability to the petty meanness of unhappy people. Never let other people convince you that feeling rubbish about yourself is the right or only response to being in contact with them. It's their feeling about themselves, so let them keep it.

4. You get the future you expect

I sometimes hear this communicated in a hippy, 'the universe will provide' kind of way. I don't mean that. I've run out of Native American stories, so let me tell you about a client whose experience is pretty typical. His name was Mr Geronimo. He had a chance of promotion. He'd had the chance before but something always seemed to hold him back. This time his partner pushed him into submitting the application. The night sweats started, and Geronimo told anyone who'd listen that he probably wouldn't get the promotion. He found himself strangely distracted when he should have been preparing. Every time he thought of the interview or someone brought it up, he got an image of him making a complete fool of himself. As the interview got closer, and his nervousness grew, this waking nightmare became more and more intense. On the day of the interview his partner had to drive him there. He visited the toilet a number of times – the last occasion to puke – before walking into the room to be met by the gaze of the inter-viewing panel. He turned into a gibbering wreck, barely capable of finishing a sentence, and the interview turned into his nightmare. He got the future he expected.

You feed what you focus on. If you let the possibility of something ahead of you going badly be the image that you focus on when you think of it, then your brain will increas-ingly treat it as the most likely future and respond accordingly by switching to protection mode. In a sense your brain can't tell the difference between something bad that's actually happening, and an event that you're imag-ining, so it gets the body to respond as if they're the same – it's why we wake up from a nightmare with a thumping heart. The adrenaline dump from this protection response will make you less yourself – **strong emotion makes you stupid** – and you won't be the best version of yourself. **Think things how you want them.** If Mr Geronimo had rehearsed in his head the interview going well, really focusing on everything about it that would make him confi-dent, his brain would have responded by releasing dopamine and he'd have felt rewarded by the thought of the interview. He would have treated it as a growth opportunity. It wouldn't guarantee him the job, but it would mean the version of him most likely to get the job turned up for the interview.

Anxiety is a fear of something that hasn't happened yet; you can't be anxious about something that's already happened. 'Ah,' I hear you say, 'I broke Mum's favourite vase last week, and I'm really anxious about that.' 'Yes', I respond, sagely stroking my white beard, 'if you knew she was never going to find out you probably wouldn't be anxious. It's the fear of what happens when she does find out that is making you suffer.' Mark Twain was one of those people who seemed to speak in useful quotes. This is one of my favourites, *'I've had a lot of worries in my life, most of which never happened.'* A century later the lead character in one of my favourite films – *Van Wilder: Party Liaison* (I've always leant towards the classical) – supported Twain with this homily, **'Worrying is like a rocking chair. It gives you something to do, but it doesn't get you anywhere.'**

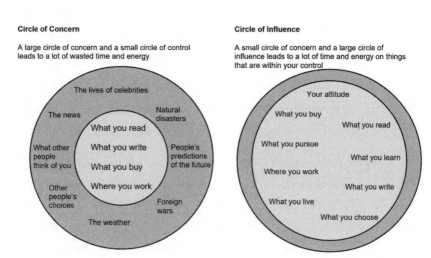

Circle of Concern

A large circle of concern and a small circle of control leads to a lot of wasted time and energy

The lives of celebrities
The news
Natural disasters
What you read
What other people think of you
What you write
People's predictions of the future
What you buy
Other people's choices
Where you work
Foreign wars
The weather

Circle of Influence

A small circle of concern and a large circle of influence leads to a lot of time and energy on things that are within your control

Your attitude
What you buy
What you read
What you pursue
What you learn
Where you work
What you write
What you live
What you choose

I wrote about this earlier in the book. Imagine you have two circles. One is your circle of influence – the things you can affect. The other is your circle of concern – the things that can be on your mind, but which you can't directly change.

There's lots of things to be concerned about, the media throw them at us every day: the environment, the government, the economy, various health scares, and world affairs. If we're not careful we can lose a lot of energy focusing on the things in our circle of concern rather than our circle of influence. This does nothing to nudge us towards growth, and it primes our brains to seek more of the same. If you focus instead on those things in your life you *can* influence, it increases your sense of empowerment. Don't confuse influence with control. I can't control the damage the human race is doing to the environment, but I can influence the damage that I do to it, and I can choose my level of involvement in influencing what is done about it – by joining environmental lobby organisations like Greenpeace, by helping my local wildlife trust, or by planting a tree in my garden. I think you'll find that by focusing on your circle of influence you begin to realise the personal power you have. It will lead you to being more proactive in life, which in turn will enlarge and enrich your world. If you can't influence it, don't concern yourself with it – you have better things to do than sit in a rocking chair.

You own a time machine. Your brain can whiz you back into the past, or shoot you into the future. Use it wisely. Every moment spent thinking about the future, or the past, is time not spent savouring the present. It's a protection device. Avoid it. Only visit the past to make yourself feel good, or to remind yourself of something about you that gives you what you need in the moment. Visualise the future how you want it before you fall asleep each night. The combination of these two habits will tune your brain towards growth. By doing so – and attending to the present – you'll become more aware of the opportunities your unconscious brings to your attention that will take you towards the future you want. Remember that you're walking down the same street as everyone else, with the same potholes to trip you up, and the same lucky pennies on the ground. Which come your way most often is mainly a product of what you expect.

5. Nobody is worth knowing who thinks what you wear matters

Adults often see the choices their children make that they disagree with as a sign of rebellion. More often they're the result of a shift in whose opinion carries most weight with them – their parents or their friends. It's actually a sign of progress if you put your friends first at some point (I'd expect it some point in your teens). Later, listening to both but deciding for yourself will be the real goal.

Similarly, the selections many make in their choice of clothing will reflect the opposite of what it might appear to be – it fulfils a need to fit in. Teenagers often like to see themselves as rebels, but the group they rarely rebel against are their own peers. Kids are desperate to fit in and, for many, the highest aspiration is to be invisible through matching to the group norm. So, while adults – or even people of their own age – might see a bunch of Goths or Emos (or whatever the counter-culture group will be when you're that age) as being rebellious, actually it's just a group of kids conforming to the norms of the group they've decided to belong to. And belonging is what it's all about. As young people begin to squirm from beneath the control of their parents, our evolution demands that we not stand alone against the world, so peer groups become extremely important. Even introverts, who will have a smaller group of friends than extroverts, will still connect strongly, if only to one or two special friends. And each group will tribalise. They'll develop a certain language, rituals, clothing preferences. There are always leaders within the group, and it's always interesting to observe how people tend to mimic their leaders. It's because **people like people who are like them.** Over millions of years, where people outside of the tribe have constituted a greater threat than those within the tribe, we've evolved this trait of finding similarity comforting, and have expressed it through an adoption of symbols of similarity – like clothing, decoration, in-humour and favourite music. With societies being hierarchical it's no wonder that the trends that tend to emerge are driven by whoever in the group is deemed to be the leader of it. Not always, but often.

When I was a boy clothing wasn't such a symbol.

Nowadays, designer labels begin with baby wear, so from the beginning children are fed the idea that this matters. This is purely my prejudice, but I'd rather wear a cheap T-shirt that says 'I'm stupid' than spend a fortune on a designer one that proves it. Pay for quality. Pay because you like it. That's completely OK. Nobody can tell you the value of something, only you can know, so if you love clothes, if you enjoy expressing yourself through them, if they're a part of the 'having fun being me' thing, then spend what you like. Just don't pay to be like other people or hope they like you more because of it.

I'm not asking this of you from the outset. Adolescence especially is a time when it's fine to wear camouflage while you get your bearings. But there will come a moment when you look around you and realise that you don't like people more because you share the same logo, and that that applies to them too. Unless you walk around in a Disney costume you really won't be liked more for what you're wearing, but for what you do. I've found the two things that have increased my popularity most are not trying to be popular and being nice. That's it. You are surrounded every day by opportunities to be kind to others, to make them feel a little happier because they crossed your path. It takes almost no effort. Notice something nice to say about them, or smile in greeting, ask how they are (and listen to the response). Open a door, help them reach for something in the supermarket. Serve. It's that simple.

Positive psychology is the study of what happy people do to be happy, and what positive psychologists have discovered is that happiness is not an accident of birth, it's the result of a way of living, and fundamental to it is serving others. If you put yourself out so that somebody else benefits, I guarantee you'll feel better for doing so. Show gratitude for what people do for you and the same thing will happen. Make kindness your designer label and you can wear a used bin bag and people will still like you and want you in their lives – and people will start wearing bin bags to try to get what you've got.

6. Sometimes what others try to teach you is because of their own stuff

I was bullied at school. Not badly. Often it was the fear that it might be my turn next that was actually what I suffered from most – hence my liking for Van Wilder's wisdom. There was one boy in my year that everyone was scared of. Some kept as far from him as possible, others became his hyenas. For a while I tried being on the edge of the pack but it just wasn't me, so in the main I used humour to divert their attention. Being bullied left me with doubts about myself – if you live in a state of protection for too long you often become a person who thinks less of themselves for being scared. It was many years before I realised it was the bully who was actually the one who was frightened.

I've said earlier in the book how we fear rejection – from our parents and from the tribe. If our experiences lead us to conclude that we're not 'ok' as a person, then we tend to defend ourselves/react in one of two ways: we protect ourselves by submission, or by aggression.

Members of the first group project an air of 'the world's OK, but I'm not'. Things are their fault, everyone else is better than they are, and better able to cope. They will tend to put other people first – to people-please. They will be poor at standing up for themselves and will often be someone's door mat. They wait to be rescued, often attaching themselves to someone who they perceive to be powerful or in a position to save them. They come into my therapy room hoping I'm going to be that person.

Then you have the people who project 'I'm ok, it's the world that's not'. These are often the bullies, the people who need to be on top, who must be right, who must make others wrong, who tell anyone who has to listen how good they are. They don't usually come to therapy, unless it's to prove that their therapist is rubbish like everyone else. Their aggression is war paint. Scratch beneath it and you'll find they're not really ok with themselves at all; their tactic is to make themselves feel better by making those around them feel worse. They try to keep their head above the water of self-hate by treading on others. Unfortunately, **behaviours driven by negative emotion tend to create what you're trying to avoid,** so their response to their self-loathing increases their self-loathing and they become more and more unhappy as the years go by – and make those submissive people attached to them feel the same, because these two types often pair up. Submissive people can be attracted by the illusory power of the aggressor and feel that they deserve no better than to be bullied. The aggressor feels more powerful by having a partner who lives in their shadow. Interestingly, if their relationship finally cracks it's the aggressor who tends to fall to pieces. The submissive has the chance to learn something from the experience that helps them move to a better position – that of an assertive person who recognises that we're all fellow strugglers.

You are going to come across people from both camps. The submissive is either going to try to convince you that you are the answer to their needs, or get you to sign up to the notion that the world is a threatening, dangerous place that will hurt you if it can. The aggressor will seek to persuade you that you are here to service their needs, that you'll never reach their standards, and that your proper place is below them. Some of your friends are going to have parents like this and you'll see the effects as your mates swallow these messages until they become true. If you befriend a submissive, don't be seduced by the service they offer you, help them discover their own worth. Your esteem will not be boosted by their slavery but by their emancipation. Be careful if you befriend an aggressor, they will wear down your confidence and try to make you equally unkind.

Research has shown that **we tend to be a composite of the five people with whom we spend most time.** Choose your friends based on this as a model. Who do I want to be, and who do I know who exemplifies these things most? People will teach you their stuff whether they mean to or not.

7. You're writing your life story. Be the character in it you want to be

Most people live as if they're following some kind of a script – and that someone else is writing it. As I said earlier, the Jesuits say give them the boy until he's seven and they will give you the man. A guy called Eric Berne reckoned that children had determined their life story by about the same age and spend the rest of their lives proving it – whether it's a good story or a horror. It's easy for our past to become our destiny, and for us to become more of what we've always been, but it doesn't have to be so.

I think one of the biggest goals of life is to take the keyboard out of the hands of this invisible scriptwriter and start defining the nature of your story and your role in it. Because we don't exist. You can dig around in your brain for as long as you like and you won't find yourself in there. I think we're just an idea the brain has that helped it plan its next move, and that idea became so developed that it saw itself in the mirror and believed in what it saw. I believe all of us are just electricity and chemicals running around our brain. If you embrace that thought – that you're just a thought – it frees you. **I believe there is no destiny other than the one you make, there is no meaning as to why you're here other than the one you give it. Nobody is watching, and nobody is judging, least of all the universe. So you can be who you choose.** That last word is the big one. Choice is your goal.

I used to think that 'personal development' would make

my problems disappear. Well, in a way I was right, because I can't even remember what I used to worry about, but new ones took their place. Like many, I hoped the sea of life would become like a mill pond. It didn't, I just learned to navigate the waves better, and that is the point of personal development – to realise that it's your hand on the tiller, it's your choice which star to navigate by, which destination to head for. Living deliberately and not surrendering control of your choices is the hardest of choices, and the one that will give you the best shot at making your life what you want it to be.

Viktor Frankl was a Jewish psychoanalyst who was sent to the concentration camps by the Nazis. He spent three years as a prisoner. He wrote of his experiences, and the learning he had taken from them, in his classic book *Man's Search for Meaning*. Please read it. The essence of it is this:

> 'The one thing you can't take away from me is the way I choose to respond to what you do to me. The last of one's freedoms is to choose one's attitude in any given circumstance.'

Nobody can tell you who your character is, or what your story is. Neither can life, but 80% of people will let it. Wake every morning and choose your attitude to your life. Be the person in your story who lives that attitude. **Practise doesn't make perfect, it makes permanent.** If you practise being the you each day who remains awake to the fact that the day you're going to have is your choice, and being the you each day who has the most fun as a result of those choices, then after a while it becomes who you are. It's a heroic choice, and most won't make it.

Ooh, and don't take yourself seriously, because you're only make-believe – like everybody else.

I love you,

Granddad x

Conclusion

I started to write a book – that sheaf of blank paper I started with – and now it sits beside me. As it's grown it's changed, just like a child. I thought it might just be about some common miseries my clients experience which I wanted to help you inoculate you and your children from. As those miseries got linked to the way our brains work, and as how our brains work connected to the way our society operates, it became something a bit bigger: the idea that changing the way you approach raising our children could actually improve you. Then it became something bigger still: changing the world itself for the better.

I'm not asking you to sign up for that as a crusade – I'm sure you have plenty of other things to fill your day – but the good thing is that you don't have to. If you spend the first year of your child's life making them secure through touch; through your reliable presence; through your words to them, and about them, being positive and loving; with your facial expressions being those of love, amusement and joy; you'll have already begun tuning their brains towards an expectation of living in a growth reality. From there, if you use their young calculations to create connections between events and their sense of ok-ness by making your explanatory style an optimistic one, you'll prime them to see opportunity everywhere. If you teach them that they're responsible for their results, and that their world will only be what they want it to be if they make it that way, then you've started them on the road to ILOC. If you encourage them in a growth mindset rather than a fixed one, they'll grow up resilient in the face of the challenges they meet, and grow persistently in response to their setbacks. If you develop in them the discipline to stick to small habits that move them forward and find intrinsic ways to motivate them, you'll be able to sit back and enjoy watching their ride – noticing that growing them has grown you too.

And if there's enough of you raising your children this way and enough of you, as families, avoiding those things in the media that spark you into protection, avoiding the siren call of consumerist badge collecting and instead give service to others, then maybe a tipping point will be reached where each of you contributes to the flapping of a new butterfly that *does* change the world into a better place.

Changing the world one child, and one parent, at a time. I like that idea.

The beginning.

Bibliography

Oliver James, *Affluenza* (Vermilion, 2007)

John Bowlby, *Attachment* (Pimlico, 1997)

Martin Seligman, *Authentic Happiness* (Nicholas Brealey Publishing, 2003)

Trevor Silvester, *Cognitive Hypnotherapy: What's that about, and how can I use it?* (Matador, 2010)

Daniel Pink, *Drive* (Canongate Books 2011)

Paul Ekman, *Emotions Revealed* (Wiedenfeld & Nicholson, 2004)

Mihaly Csikszentmihalyi, *Finding Flow* by (Basic Books, 1998)

Jean Twenge, *Generation Me* (Free Press, 2007)

Robert Cialdini, *Influence – The Psychology of Persuasion* (1st Collins Business Essentials, 2007)

James Clear, *Transform Your Habits* (www.jamesclear.com)

Trevor Silvester, *Lovebirds* by Trevor Silvester (Coronet, 2013)

Carol Dweck, *Mindset* (Robinson, 2012)

Cass Sunstein, *Nudge* (Penguin, 2009)

Robert Anton Wilson, *Prometheus Rising* (Hilaritas Press LLC, 2016)

Alain de Botton, *Status Anxiety* (Penguin, 2005)

Timothy Ferris, *The Four Hour Body* (Vermilion, 2011)

Bruce Lipton PhD, *The Biology of Belief* (Hay House, 2005)

Norman Doidge, *The Brain That Changes Itself* (Penguin, 2008)

Thomas Metzinger, *The Ego Tunnel* (Basic Books, 2009)

Jean Piaget, *The Language and Thought of a Child* (Routledge, 2001)

Susan Blackmore, *The Meme Machine* (Oxford University Press, 2000)

Ryan Holiday, *The Obstacle is the Way* (Profile Books, 2005)

Charles Duhigg, (Cornerstone, 2013)

Daniel Gardner, *The Science of Fear* (Plume Books, 2009)

Jeff Olson, *The Slight Edge* (Success Books, 2005

Tor Norretranders, *The User Illusion* (Penguin, 1999)

Daniel Kahneman, *Thinking Fast and Slow* (Penguin, 2012)

Joe Simpson, *Touching the Void* (Vintage, 1998)

Gil Boyne, *Transforming Therapy* (Westwood)

Read Montague, *Why Choose this Book?* (EP Dutton & Co, 2006)

Kary Mullis, *Dancing Naked in the Mind Field* (Bloomsbury Publishing, 2000)

Marco Iacoboni, *Mirroring People* (Farrar Straus Giroux, 2008)

Dr John Ratey & Eric Hagerman, *Spark* (*Little Brown and Company,* 2008)

Malcolm Gladwell, *Outliers* (Penguin, 2009)

Thomas A Harris, *I'm OK, You're OK* (Arrow, 2012)

Viktor Frankl, *Man's Search for Meaning* (Rider, 2004)

Hugh Macleod, *Ignore Everybody* (Portfolio, 2009)

Acknowledgements

I always leave this part of the book until last. I never truly know who I'm going to be grateful for until I've finished it because help always appears from unexpected quarters. It's also a useful way of reminding myself that, while writing a book is largely a solitary experience, where a book comes from is never a single mind.

With this particular book, who else could I begin my thanks than with my own children? I have two great sons, Mark and Stuart. They both make me laugh, which I value so much, and they both support Chelsea, which is a sign I got something right. Now they have children of their own they're both showing me that I was obviously a slow learner when I was in their position. They've taken to it in a way that's made me so proud, and, as Granddad, I hope they know I've got their backs.

Next has to come the new joys in my life, my grandchildren Heath, Sasha and Seth. Heath is the son of Mark and his wife Tara. When I began thinking about this book, Heath was yet to arrive, and now, as this is the last part of the book I write, Heath has entertained us for nearly five years. His escapades, or sometimes just his smile via photos sent to us on WhatsApp, have brightened many a cold morning. Sasha, the daughter of Stuart and his wife Ksenia, is something completely new to my experience – a little girl. Beautiful, brave, and a complete mystery. I think her little finger is going to become a familiar place for me. And now, a year ago, she was joined by a baby brother, Seth, for whom giggling crazily seems to be his default response to most of his day. They're proof that love just expands infinitely. All of them give me so much to look forward to.

As ever, my clients remain the biggest sources of learning in my life, and I want to thank all of them for what they've given me. It takes courage to change, and I spend a lot of time with some very brave people. Those from Kids Company have been a source of wonder at the resilience of the human spirit and the power of hope. I was proud to be a part of it and heartbroken at its demise.

If my students read this book they'll find themselves in familiar territory, and so they should, because so often it's been in front of them that the philosophy that drives this book, and the phrases and mantras that pepper it, have emerged. I'm very lucky to attract as my students people who inspire me to teach Cognitive Hypnotherapy, and who go on so often to do wonderful work with it. Seeing where this shared journey takes us is a truly exciting prospect.

My test-readers occupy a special place in the process of writing a book – a painful place, but absolutely essential. Each reads it and shreds it in different ways, leaving me with three versions of why it's not good enough yet. And from that, and the tatters of my self-belief as a writer, something better finally emerges. If you don't like it, it really wasn't their fault, they did their best with what I gave them. Jan, Ruth and Cat, thank you so much. And then, when I thought I was finished, my brilliant editor Saethryd Brandreth was only just beginning. She took that manuscript, put it through another blender, and what you're reading finally emerged. I really am more grateful than I probably appeared at the time.

It has been a real growth experience for me to have had the chance to learn about the publishing world under the tutelage of my publisher and editor, Mark Booth. His quiet belief in me, his subtle advice, his less than subtle advice, and his tenacity in making this book be the best it could be, has been more appreciated than he can ever know. And the lovely team at Hodder, who do so much to bring the book into the place where you found it, are great people who actually make meetings quite fun to be in. With good biscuits.

Finally, my thanks to the three people I share my life with. First, my wife, Bex. We became a couple just as I found my way, and I don't for a moment think that was a coincidence. She is my best friend, advisor and confidante (I'd include lover but my kids will read this and think that's icky), as well as being tremendously forgiving of my many faults. I know she's aware of them because she's made a list. Thank goodness that, when I ignored the fact she'd declared her feelings for me during a conversation, I had the sense to stammer a few minutes later . . . 'that thing you said . . . should we talk about that?' Lord knows what she'd have done without me if I hadn't. Better, probably.

The last two come as a pair. Out of a tragedy we ended up with two dogs, miniature Schnauzers called Fred and Betty. The sum is so much more than the parts. They comprise the bulk of our conversations, and provide a disproportionate amount of the fun, laughter and mess. Literally as I wrote this, Fred came dancing past the door with the door mat in his mouth. In the magic way that dogs have, they effortlessly remind us of how easy it is to grow when you focus on what really matters. Although why they think that what really matters is eating sheep's poo is completely beyond us.